1998

# If You Want to Make GOD
# *REALLY* Laugh,
## Show Him Your Business Plan

# If You Want to Make GOD
# *REALLY* Laugh,
## Show Him Your Business Plan

### The 101 Universal Laws of Business

## Barry J. Gibbons

**AMACOM**
**American Management Association**
New York • Atlanta • Boston • Chicago • Kansas City • San Francisco • Washington, D.C.
Brussels • Mexico City • Tokyo • Toronto

Library of Congress Cataloging-in-Publication Data
    Gibbons, Barry J.
        If you want to make GOD really laugh, show him your business plan:
        the 101 universal laws of business / Barry J. Gibbons.
            p.    cm.
        Includes bibliographical references and index.
        ISBN 0-8144-0498-7
        1. Success in business.   2. Strategic planning.   3. Business
    planning.   4. Industrial management.   I. Title.
    HF5386.G36      1999
    658.4´012—DC21                                                          98-50495
                                                                               CIP

Printing number
10   9   8   7   6   5   4   3   2   1

*To Judy, Jon, and Ben. For keeping me grinning.*

Would you please all be upstanding for the singing of capitalism's universal hymn, *Summam Scrutemur*?[1] It is to be found on page 322 of your hymn books, and the melody will be Beethoven's *Ode to Joy*. Music will be provided by the IBM String Quartet.

Jesus, help me through next quarter,
I need profits like a rock.
If I don't make what I oughtta,
Christ, I'll have to dump some stock!

*(Chorus)*    *I have frozen all expenses,*
*Air travel now is totally banned.*
*Marketing costs are all past tenses,*
*But earnings will come in as planned.*

We believe that we *empower,*
And our folks are energized.
But if you're not paid by the hour,
Chances are you'll be downsized.

*(Chorus)*    *I have frozen all expenses (etc.)* . . .

Auditors have signed our books off,
Our accounts complete and formal.
When the senior partner . . . er . . . leaves
Then we can get back to normal.

*(Chorus)*    *I have frozen all expenses* . . .

Restructuring plans are now completed,
To better serve our customers dear.
Although they'll be quite gen'rously treated,
5000 employees are leaving here.

*(Finale)*    *I have frozen all expenses* . . .

Please be seated. Let us pray.

---

[1]Let's look at the bottom line.

# CONTENTS

# The 101 Universal Laws of Business

# Acknowledgment

My *profound* thanks are offered to Caroline Carney, my literary agent, who received a very badly thrown ball and ran with it. And to Ellen Kadin and the team at AMACOM, who insisted they were right when they were.

# If You Want to Make GOD
# *REALLY* Laugh,
## Show Him Your Business Plan

# Introduction

We're given a lot of free room to make a mess of it, but in reality most of our existence is governed by a series of universal laws. Some—like death, gravity, and the magnetic north—were spotted early and have been thoroughly researched and proven beyond challenge. Others clearly exist but are waiting for a serious academic mind to provide quantitative proof. An example of one of these is: *An American citizen will never walk up a moving escalator.* I have observed this for over thirty years and although it is unlikely to land me my (so far) elusive Nobel prize, you can trust me on it.

These laws do not just apply to the seminal things in life (death, escalators, etc.). They also rule many of the discretionary, everyday things we do, such as buying a bottle of wine. Here several universal laws come into play, but the main one is: *A $10 bottle of wine is better than a $5 dollar bottle, but not twice as good.*[1] This law applies all the way up the price scale.

There are millions of these laws at work in the world of business and they are important to all of us. As Woodrow Wilson pointed out: "Business underlies everything in our national life, including our spiritual life." Some of the laws, however, are trivial in the extreme and will have no place in this

---

[1]Wine buying is subject to other universal rules—e.g., *If the label has a picture on it, the content is usually crappy.*

book. Here I am thinking of universal laws of the kind that state: *If you leave your paper clips in a container overnight, when you pick one to use in the morning it will have mated with at least another five and you will be faced with an unusable tiny mass of inextricably linked steel.* No, I will rise above that kind of light-weight subject matter and deal with the laws that apply in more profound areas. There are more than enough of those, and the business world surely needs a critical academic analysis of them all because it is in a mess. A shambolic, poorly directed, depressing *mess*. And that's just General Motors.

It was never meant to be this way. In all fairness, God (and please, mentally insert the name of your own deity here; I want no fatwas) should be given reasonable marks for the whole Creation thing. Of course it is easy, with hindsight, to criticize—that the provision of wash basins, for example, wasn't in line with that required by the permitting code for such a construction job. It is also easy to suggest He put in a couple of deliberate errors, such as telling us in the Operations Manual that there are only two sexes when there are clearly at least five.[2] Despite all this, and the fact that if He was going to do it again He'd probably run a small test project first before going for the really big one, the project scored well and generally ran to plan[3] in its early days. Until business came along. Then it was downhill all the way.

When it first emerged in recognizable form in the Middle Ages, business was no more than an extension of the social dimensions of the community. The word *company* actually derives from the concept of taking bread together (from the Latin *cum panis*) and I don't know about you, but that sounds just fine to me. Yet if we press the fast forward button to the late twentieth century and then press the play button, we see a very different picture. See if any of the following ring a bell with you:

| | |
|---|---|
| Complex | Hierarchical |
| Paranoid | Regimented |
| Antisocial | Bureaucratic |

[2]An unconfirmed sixth was spotted in South Miami Beach recently. Still to be ratified.

[3]Notwithstanding a small glitch in the script with the Israelites.

| | |
|---|---|
| Pressured | Fatiguing |
| Tense | Routine (boring) |
| Destructive | Wrong things centralized |
| No smoking | Wrong things decentralized |
| No smiling | Impersonal |

That list took me about thirty seconds to compile. In another thirty seconds, you could add at least five more of your own. (Go on, I'll wait). Okay, stop now. I said, *stop*. *Dilbert*'s raison d'etre is illustrating all these ills and many more in his wonderfully loopy but stereotypical workplace. His creator, Scott Adams, is besieged on the Internet with literally thousands of additional mind-boggling examples. If you have worked for AT&T in the last few years you probably have ticked off this list and added a few more before your morning coffee break.

Clearly God, when he reviews the whole world project, will pause and reflect. Luckily, some of the things he got wrong were able to be corrected fairly quickly with a bit of tweaking (for example, the fate of the American buffalo, the Black Death, Communism, and the launch of New Coke). But easy fixes do not apply when it comes to business. This particular boat has a hole below the water line.

From the outset, this book sides with the theory that the way modern business has evolved is one of God's top three surviving mistakes, along with France and cobras. It chews up at least a third of the life of most people in it and, for most people, the negatives usually outweigh the positives in the overall experience, by a distance. Over the last two or three decades business has become riddled with stupid counterforces and paradoxes that go beyond self-destruction and now often threaten the sanity of the people involved. Let's just pick four, and we can begin to see where the Divine afflatus started to go wrong:

◆ Today's cluttered, competitive markets need distinct, added-value products and services. What has evolved instead? A planet full of boring, ho-hum goods.

- The new dynamics of corporate change means we need faster decision making. What has happened is that access to (almost) infinite data banks and analysis has enabled us to procrastinate with real sophistication.

- Of the one hundred largest economies in the world today, almost exactly half are corporations. However, of the fifty or so countries on that list, only a couple are not democracies. *None* of the corporations are. Just imagine the impact if one of the countries expelled (i.e., downsized) several tens or even hundreds of thousands of its citizens.

- Whether you employ thousands of people or three, you need them to be savvy and motivated. What have we got? The most alienated workforces *ever*.

Is it any wonder that leaders look like idiots and the led look confused? The bad news is that we can't look to the business schools to help us through, because all but the best of them actually perpetuate the problem. Behind most of their walnut lecterns are professorial minds, blunted by the comfort of tenured employment[4] and unsullied by real-world experience, still pumping out drivel about an individual's hierarchical needs. The individual in question, of course, is far more concerned with car lease payments.

Our role models in business don't help us either. It is hard not to agree with England's late Lord George Brown (a noted, postwar ebullient[5] Labour politician) when he called them "the Lords of Misrule." The fat-cat corporate icons earning multimillions are too far out of sight for most of us to ape them, even if we wanted to. If we look to Wall Street, there is little positive or attractive about the elitist parasites we'll find. Most middle managers simply haven't the stomach to follow the path to stardom of the corporate downsizing mass murderers. Please note that in this paragraph on corporate role models, I am leav-

---

[4]Talking of God's bigger mistakes, tenured employment is right up there with tofu.

[5]He drank a lot.

---

ing aside all reference and comparison to Bill Gates, because I believe it makes sense to limit this work to the planet Earth. I am unshakable in my belief that he arrived from someplace else.

It is also no good looking to the ordinary Joe or Janet for anchor points, because they are all over the place. If you saw two stone cutters doing exactly the same work and asked them what they were doing, one would define it as cutting stone into blocks while the other would probably spout on about being a member of a diverse group adding value to reusable resources while pursuing the success criteria of building a cathedral.

Just where did all these stupid theories come from? Who originated the "circumcision theory"of cost cutting?[6] What's with the league tables? Can you imagine the nightmare of having your company ranked as number 501 by *Fortune*?

Is there any way we can bring order to the chaos? Thankfully, I believe there is. In the same way that universal laws govern our existence, I believe a series of universal laws exists in business. Some are easy to categorize (i.e., you can't break them and expect to live). Others might seem less intimidating but you ignore them also at your peril. Over their range they have very little in common, except that you can't play at them (you must be prepared to inhale), and it seems to me that a working knowledge of all of them is a must-have for a ride through this white water.

I'll take an example from the very essence of this thing we call business to illustrate the point. Almost all companies take time out now and again to put together a business plan. For the big outfits this can be a huge, expensive exercise involving blue-chip consultants, with the resulting document (when it has been nicely bound by the PR agency) weighing as much as five or six pounds without appendices. For the small business, it might be a two-page semiliterate offering put together for the bank. For the project team it might be a tight project plan with well-defined goals and success criteria. For all of them it is a

---

[6]Cut off 10% and throw it away ...

thought-through reflection on how the situation looks today and a judgement on what will happen next.

At this stage we must remember that God has given every indication he is now playing business for laughs—accepting the fact that nothing much else is going on today that brings a smile to his face (although the MIR space station and Woody Allen's sex life have provided him with some comic relief).

Now, just imagine that God could see your business plan. Somehow or other—using fax, UPS, or E-mail[7]—you got a copy of your precious seminal document to him. I believe he would have his biggest laugh since the fall of Rome. Your outline of the current state of the business is funny enough, containing as it does at least two of the fundamental paradoxes I have already noted. But the plan for the future is the real doozy. You see, he **knows** what is coming down the pike, and your version of it is just so, so funny.

This leads to an important (and our first) universal law: When you have completed, bound, and presented your business plan to the appropriate audience, it contains the one and only scenario that is guaranteed not to happen. It is critical to know and understand this for two reasons. First, some businesspeople, including yours truly, have found this an extremely helpful planning base in its own right. Second—this is a wee bit more obtuse, but also very important—it helps you differentiate leaders from managers. This is an

**Universal Law #1**

*When you have completed, bound, and presented your business plan to the appropriate audience, it contains the one and only scenario that is guaranteed not to happen.*

issue that has confused everyone in business since business began (with Windows 2500 BC): Just what makes a leader, and why are they so different from the thousands, millions, of ordinary businesspeople who set out with them on the same mission? Whereas management is simply a profession, leadership is

[7]Him@aol.com

clearly a condition.[8] One way to spot leadership is to monitor how the individual handles the business plan and our first universal law. The manager, you see, lives and believes in The Plan. Once it is signed off, he or she monitors it closely (albeit with an increasingly wrinkled brow) and tries to make it happen. The leader, however, returns from the business plan presentation, sticks the document in a cupboard with all the others, digests the fact that at least there is a clear knowledge of what *won't* happen, and prepares to get to the end of the first street, peer round the corner, and deal with what actually comes up.

You get the idea, right? These universal laws apply across a wide range of business locations and activities. Whether you work for a mighty corporation or run a small business selling a household service, their forces apply. Some of them appear weird at first (such as the need to avoid tidy graveyards), but these universal law jumped out at me during nearly thirty corporate years. I have recently developed them in business seminars with some of the biggest corporate names on both sides of the Atlantic and noted how these laws have consistently struck a chord with a wide variety of business delegates.

I have deliberately ranged across a wide variety of topics and disciplines in writing this book. My own experience has been wide ranging, and neither the sources nor uses of these laws can or should be constrained to one area or level of business.

But, dear reader, I must warn you: I get deflected. Maybe it is the Irish blood in me, but one of the reasons I chose to quit big business was that I had stopped enjoying it. It is probably a fair criticism of my career that I laughed too much. I can only offer the weak defense that I worked with so many wonderful people and saw so much that was just so...well...*funny.* When I felt the joy running out I left big business, setting myself the strict life goals of only getting involved with projects that I

---

[8]The nearest I got to defining this further is linking it to the role of the queen bee. She exudes a chemical substance that holds the system together and is responsible for the spirit of the hive. Before you say anything, I agree this doesn't work using H. Ross Perot as an example, but exceptions sometimes prove the rule.

enjoy and of getting to know one less person every day. This book has failed when it came to the latter goal, so it has survived because it has been a labor of love, which means I've had a lot of fun. In turn, this means you will be invited to join me in some rather strange deflections, such as my concern as to what happened to the (male) nipples in the movie *Pocahontas* and my tracking of the pulse rate of the three-toed sloth during orgasm. The latter is critically important to an understanding of some new universal laws concerning customer service. I also ponder the fate of a proposed World War II battleship made from ice.

You have been warned, but I am now ready if you are. In the words of the famous Roman senator in 42 BC: *"Me transmitte sursum,Caledoni!"*[9]

*Barry Gibbons*
*Miami, Florida, 1999*
*GibbonFile@aol.com*

---

[9]Beam me up, Scotty.

# 1

# On Tests of Rightness
# (TOR)

The universal laws in this chapter are really statements of the blindingly obvious, but my experience is that if your car isn't working, it's good to check the basics first in the hope that the discovery of a problem there will lead to an easy and full solution. Which shows you how much I know about cars.[1]

In his masterpiece, *1984*, George Orwell defined *double-think* as "the power of holding two contradictory beliefs in one's mind simultaneously, and accepting both of them." In itself it is a useful tool in describing some business experiences—such as the feeling you get when you lose a large block of un-backed-up work on your PC—but I want to introduce a concept that is much more relevant our journey. I call it *doubleact*, and I define it as "the process of mature, civilized human beings (spouses, parents, loved ones, community members, whatever) turning into lying, insensitive, economically challenged, abusive morons the minute they enter the workplace."

---

[1]You could add women and Lotus Notes to this list.

You see examples of doubleacting everywhere in business: We encourage risk taking, then punish mistakes; we champion teamwork, then reward individuals who stand out in the crowd. People who are pillars of society lie without a second thought, and official communications in particular are often hilariously untrue ("Our employees' interests have never been more in line with our shareholders' interests"[2]). Folks who exemplify prudent housekeeping spend the company's money in ways that would embarrass a kid in the mall.

None of this should surprise us; it is simply further evidence of God's sense of humor. It was he, remember, who made Beethoven so deaf that Beethoven thought he was actually a painter. Whatever the reason, something happens to us when we go to work, and we start doing wrong things. We are, of course, encouraged to do so by history, circumstances, and other people, and sometimes (God help us) we do the wrong things for the right reasons. But we do 'em all right: hundreds, thousands of them every year.

I am not talking about making mistakes. That is an entirely different science, and it is a difference we need to reflect on for a moment so we can clear the path ahead.

A lot of you have had one of those moments when you slammed a door behind you, stared at an empty room (maybe your office), and shivered with the dawning realization that you had just committed the biggest faux pas in the history of civilization. Join the club. I'm a founding member.

Some of our industrial-strength errors are, of course, a source of amusement for others. I still laugh, for instance, at the 1960s European brand manager who oversaw a launch of his brand of instant coffee in Brazil without discovering beforehand that the brand name was Portuguese slang for a specific part of the female genitals (true story).[3]

Well, we can all relax. When it comes to major league SNAFUs, none of us is in the running. Barbara Tuchman, in her

---

[2]Communication by Chemical Bank in 1995—issued simultaneously with 12,000 layoffs from the Chase Manhattan/Chemical merger.

[3]I have often wondered about the mind-set of customers who actually bought a packet of this coffee. Just what did they think they were buying?

---

magnificent work on the history of mistakes,[4] ranks 'em all. The winner—narrowly beating the behavior of the Renaissance popes—is the decision by the German High Command, made in 1916, to resume unrestricted submarine warfare. This had been halted after the *Lusitania* outrage a year before but, under increasing internal pressure to deal the Allies a mortal blow and having been advised by Field Marshal Hindenberg that his army could "take care of America," the Kaiser made the fateful decision. Tuchman ranks mistakes by their consequences, and this one brought the U.S. speedily into the war. Without America's involvement there would probably have been an impasse and an eventual (exhausted) peace on more or less equal terms. With America in the war, there was victory—followed by reparations, war guilt, Hitler, the Second World War, and 55 million dead. Now *that's* a failure.

If you let this logic run on a bit it's amazing what you can blame on the Kaiser. Apart from the fact it is now clear he was responsible for my failing a whole bunch of high school exams (Why didn't my parents realize this?), it seems obvious with hindsight that he was also responsible for the recent upward drift in my body fat percentage.[5]

Sadly, it is unlikely that anything we do will be studied by students who, in future centuries, will be charged with tracking the descent of humanity. You can relax: Your ill-fated decision to move Bill from the widget development team and put him into finance may have been a doozy, but it won't entertain your great-grandchildren. Making mistakes is part and parcel of business life. In a healthy company it is encouraged in a controlled way and is an essential ingredient in forward progress.

Doing wrong things is different from making mistakes. It is based on the assumption that most of us do right things in our parallel, nonbusiness lives, and that if we paused and

[4]*The March of Folly*, (Ballantine Books, 1985). Now, hear me: If Western business schools would abandon the dogmatic drivel they normally teach and devote at least one semester to this book and its derived implications for management, they would send out a bunch of *wise* graduates.

[5]It is now at an all-time high of 0.09 percent. If you ever meet me, remind me to check this. I may have the decimal point wrong.

reflected we would recognize that. These wrong things qualify by failing simple tests of rightness.

I have always applied Tests of Rightness (TOR) to my primary activities in business. It's a simple process of taking a few minutes to stand back and ignore all the momentum, process, noise, analysis, and data, and to ask: Does this *feel* right? Is this actually *civilized*? It is astonishing how many times we do things in a way that challenges the ascent of humanity.

**Universal Law #2**

*Deal with people individually as if you were dealing with your favorite sister. If you don't have a favorite sister, then the hell with it—imagine* **yourself** *on the receiving end.*

Let's start with the area where most businesspeople stumble most often: dealing with other people on an individual basis. Here, my universal law is simple: Deal with people individually as if you were dealing with your favorite sister. If you don't have a favorite sister, then the hell with it—imagine *yourself* on the receiving end. Trust me, you will not have to search far to find vivid examples of this TOR being broken a million times every day. My local newspaper, for instance, recently told of the shambles of a downsizing at the South Florida Miami Dade Community College. Economic pressures were such that a number of quite deep cuts were made—but that's not my issue here. It ain't fun, but sometimes external circumstances or self-inflicted wounds (or both) necessitate the need for such action. My bile rose when I saw how the individuals were treated *after* the decisions were made. A thirty-one-year coach (that's thirty-one years in the job, not thirty-one years old) learned of his department's closure, *and his own firing,* by voice mail. Another senior coach was fired by fax, *with his name spelled incorrectly.* However difficult and traumatic the circumstances, the SOBs who "managed" these processes failed the TOR. They would simply not treat their own kith and kin in that way, but it was just fine to deal with these "lesser" folk like that. If they themselves had been handled this way they would have been devastated.

The thorny subject of downsizing (or mass firing, to give it its correct name) also needs a TOR. The debate on whether or not it should happen is irrelevant. It has happened, it is still happening, and it will continue to happen, probably even picking up speed. The march of technology and the globalization of markets and production sourcing mean that fewer people will be needed and they'll be needed in different places. So downsizing becomes like terrorism: a real pain in the ass, but one we've gotta get used to, and learn to manage.

So, a lot of people are going to have to be fired—hundreds, thousands, millions of 'em. It is not a task that most people find pleasant and the danger is that the latent civilized element in most of us can lead to a fudged solution if we are faced with having to do a lot of it. If 5000 people need to go, then firing only 3000 because you are softhearted is not the correct business solution, nor does it pass our test of rightness. The universal law here is: Ruthless in decision, but gentle in execution. Define what has to be done, in great detail and without compromise, but then don't try to implement it in twenty-four hours. You will probably find your business will perform better through this period of change if you don't go cold turkey, and you can be more sensitive to those people affected by the changes. In this instance the implementation itself needs planning just as carefully as the detailed decision. If you are honest with people and indicate you can be flexible in execution in a way that helps both the continuing business *and* those people adversely affected, you can find the right path through the maze. It needn't cost much cash, and usually an accounting charge taken for "restructuring" can defend profitability during delayed implementation of a clearly defined solution. But by taking some time and by using some thought, consideration, empathy, and a small amount of resource, you pass the test of rightness.

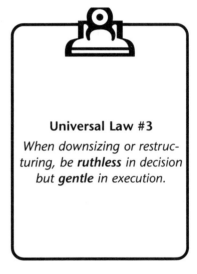

**Universal Law #3**

*When downsizing or restructuring, be **ruthless** in decision but **gentle** in execution.*

What does all this mean if you are a victim of mass firing? Let's say you know the decision has been made, you know your compensation (if any) is nonnegotiable, and you know there are so many of you that you are just a name or number to the corporate elite (a description that, I guess, covers most people in this situation). Even so, wouldn't you still hope to be treated with dignity? Wouldn't you still hope you found out before your peers, friends, and family? You'd still hope that somebody (your boss, supervisor?) would have the courage and care to tell you personally. You'd hope like hell (if you were me) to receive the news in private so you could take the hit and emotionally regroup without the benefit of an audience. You'd hope somebody would explain to you exactly what you are (and aren't) entitled to, and what it does (and doesn't) mean. None of this takes hours or thousands of dollars. It does take thinking about and planning. It takes enlightened management, at a time when enlightened management is right alongside the giant panda and the white tiger on the road to extinction.

This particular TOR doesn't just apply to mass firings—in fact it's hard to know where it stops and starts. On hitting Scott Paper, Albert Dunlap (during one of his bad hair days) instantly axed $5 million in corporate charitable contributions, citing the new constitutional seventh amendment as cause : "It is not our money to play with." This is not the time or place to offer other than a summary view on corporate charitable contributions[6] or Dunlap[7], but it is the place to comment on any management team, for any reason, suddenly stopping $5 million worth of charitable programs after you have built them up under your corporate brand name (and with it the responsibility to people who have come to rely on it.) Can you imagine the cold turkey effect of that act on folks who simply do not deserve to be dumped on like that? There's a real good chance that people could die as a result. Does Dunlap really believe his beloved stockholders want their earnings per share that way? Make your ruthless decision to cease contributions if you must, but get

[6]I am in favor.

[7]I am not in favor.

there in bite-sized chunks, letting or getting somebody else to try to fill the hole while you withdraw.

Tests of rightness also apply to the managing of monetary matters. I am continually astonished to see the prudence and common-sense practices that most people exhibit in their non-business lives vanish when they come to work. Let's start with investment decisions that, in effect, involve spending somebody else's money on projects. This science can become unreal[8] when decisions are made by weighing a project's merits by comparing them only against other projects that are jostling for position in your approved capital or expense budgets. This runs

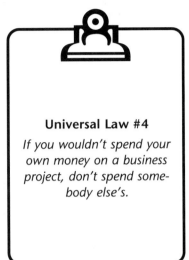

counter to the correct TOR, which insists that the alternative to spending on the project is to leave the money in the bank and do nothing. Another universal law emerges that ignores all other rival claims for the money and forces you to apply the same judgment you do when you look at a potential new car and then at your own bank balance: If you wouldn't spend your own money on a business project, don't spend somebody else's.

Systems and technology are areas of spending where business fails a similar TOR again and again. Of course, many investments in these areas have paid back a millionfold. But many more investments have been made in upgrades and developments because they were *available*, not because they were *needed*, and without any solid logic about where the incremental cash flow was going to come from to service the investment cost. I have been associated with three major retailing companies in over thirty years in business and I have witnessed millions of pounds' and dollars' worth of investments fail this TOR. Managers invested in new or upgraded retail systems without

---

[8]It's a bit like your first credit card—particularly the honeymoon period before the bill arrives. Oh, happy memories....

identifying returns or assigning accountability and responsibility for delivering them. Investment in retail systems can justify itself in a host of ways including increased sales, better inventory control, saved overhead, and many more; but to corral all the benefits you need to obey the law: Tangible investments must reap tangible returns. That means you must define the returns in advance and hold somebody accountable for their delivery. This law is becoming increasingly important as intellectual capital represents a larger and larger portion of the assets of many companies. Like any other assets, intellectual capital needs investments for both growth and maintenance, and the accountancy profession is about 150 years away from figuring out how to handle that. The key is to judge spending with the same "affordability versus potential return" analysis that management seem to apply every week in their home lives.[9]

You can use TOR in all sorts of places, and one particularly fertile area is to stop the widespread practice of good, old-fashioned lying.

Make no mistake about it, everybody in business does it. Folks who go ballistic when their kids get caught weaving a minor untruth drive into work the next day and create tapestries of misinformation and deceit. We should all be forever grateful to Scott Adams (the *Dilbert* and *Dogbert* cartoon creator) for crystallizing the most popular management lies of all time:

1. Employees are our most valuable assets.
2. I have an open-door policy.
3. You could earn more money under the new plan.
4. The future is bright.

[9]For the male of the species I exclude the purchase of boats from this thesis, where the average transaction is backed by a piece of financial logic that defies belief. I dunno about you, but I am becoming more despairing about (we) males than ever.

5. We reward risk takers.

6. Performance will be rewarded.

7. We don't shoot the messenger.

8. Training is a high priority.

9 We are reorganizing to better serve our customers.

10. I haven't heard any rumors.

11. We'll review your performance in six months.

12. Our people are the best.

13. Your input is important to us.[10]

Scott's purpose in making this list was so that we can all simply refer to the lies by their appropriate numbers and save a lot of time, which we can then use for whining. All of us could add a few of our own favorites, in my case the long-running gem authored by Big Tobacco: "We do not believe nicotine to be addictive." Wow. Just what kind of force is at work here that makes, say, a slightly balding man with a dark jacket, nice brief-case, polished shoes, two kids in private school, and a position in the church behave like this? This is a guy who probably sprays the lavatory with air freshener before he dumps just to make sure he offends and embarrasses nobody. Then he goes to work and behaves like Hitler's spin doctor.

The average annual company report—*the* corporate com-munication of the year—is a wonderful game reserve for lies, usually stringing at least five of the thirteen most popular ones together, along with a few originals to complete the picture. It often then adds something like: "The last year can best be described by the words of the immortal Charles Dickens: 'It was the best of times, it was the worst of times.'" What really hap-pened was that sales tanked, costs soared, the CEO banked a $4 million bonus, and earnings per share went negative.

I hate this side of business. I can live with spin doctors when their job is managing optics and not lying. Sir Michael Havers, a British civil servant, was accused of lying during an investigation into government actions to suppress the publica-

[10]Scott Adams, *The Dilbert Principle* (HarperCollins, 1996)

**Universal Law #6**

*If this business communica-
tion wouldn't fool your
mother, start again.*

tion of a book by a British spy. He denied it, coining the wonderful expression in his defense that he had "been economical the truth," and I can also live with that. But crossing the line into deceit cannot do anything but damage the business and the perpetrator. I offer a simple universal law that should govern all your business communications: If this wouldn't fool your mother, start again.

High up there with corporate lying in the list of deadly sins that fail TOR is abuse. Although we are flattening organizational structures, business is still hierarchical and its atomic structure is still centered around boss–subordinate relationships, an area where I believe personal abuse of every kind is rampant. Columbia University psychologist Harvey Hornstein estimates in his disturbing study of managerial abuse[11] that 90 percent of the U.S. workforce has at some time been subjected to abusive behavior, and that as many as one in five suffer every day. I have seen no objective research that counters these horrifying figures, and I know from my own experience that abuse is both extensive and one of business' best-kept secrets. Although the threat of lawsuits and the advent of enlightened processes in some companies (e.g., allowing everyone to have a mentor relationship with a senior member of the company other than their boss) have helped to curb some abuse, other recent developments such as E-mail actually enhance the opportunities for new, virulent forms of abuse.

This fails every test of rightness there is. Companies that harbor abusive managers run a huge risk of incurring punitive legal damages as well as managing a shell-shocked, less productive workforce. Constant vigilance is needed to root out abusers, and I believe the situation is serious enough to warrant two universal

[11]*Brutal Bosses and Their Prey* (Riverhead Books, 1995).

laws. The first one is: Every employee should have a mentor as well as a boss.

The second law recognizes that abuse only occurs when a vertical organizational structure provides one human being with power over another. When businesses were largely people-heavy and low-tech, hierarchical span-breaking structures had to be the order of the day. No more: If an organizational layer cannot clearly add value to the business, do without it. If it is marginal, the benefits of not having it outweigh the risks of having it.

I'll finish my discussion of TOR with a look at the relationship with the customer: that gullible, lemming-like creature who forks out a chunk of post-tax income on your company's good or services.

Thanks to the wonders of laptop computers, I am writing this on a Lufthansa flight, one of four I have made with the airline during a trip from the U.S. to Germany. Of the four flights, three were delayed (one badly enough to cause me to miss a connection) and one was canceled, but that is not my problem. I have traveled enough to know that delays and cancellations are very rarely the responsibility of the folks you deal with immediately, and in fact they are often not the responsibility of the airline itself. I have also learned that getting mad every time your plane is delayed (or about anything completely beyond your control) is a fast track way to requiring bypass surgery.[12]

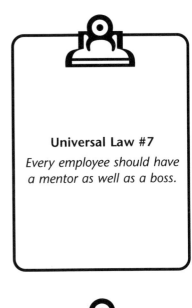

**Universal Law #7**
*Every employee should have a mentor as well as a boss.*

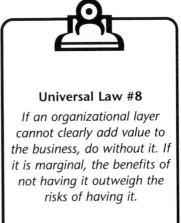

**Universal Law #8**
*If an organizational layer cannot clearly add value to the business, do without it. If it is marginal, the benefits of not having it outweigh the risks of having it.*

---

[12]Travel tip: What I normally do to ease these tensions is travel with a small goat. If things get rough I sacrifice it as an offering to St. Christopher, and this usually does the trick (although you should be warned that the process can make a bit of a mess, and they get a bit annoyed if you do it in the executive lounges in the airports).

My problem with Lufthansa concerned the dozen or so airline staff I asked for information or help at varying points in this tortured round trip. I know they didn't necessarily realize I was traveling first class and had paid roughly the equivalent of the GDP of a mid-size third world country for the ticket. I know some of them were hassled with all the delays, but for all that I was a teensy-weensy bit unhappy to be treated like an mosquito by most of them. Trust me.

When we're dealing with TOR relating to customers, there is no need to focus on the specification of the product or service offering. That is about determining the cocktail mix of product, price, and service that you offer the marketplace, and the universal laws about that are handled in another part of this book. What we need to concentrate on here is what happens when you don't deliver on spec, because that's when you do wrong things.

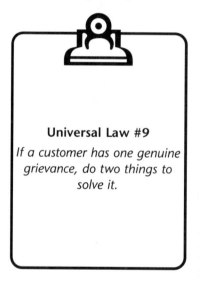

**Universal Law #9**

*If a customer has one genuine grievance, do two things to solve it.*

If a customer has invested in your offering and you have not delivered, you are presented with two things: first, a blow to both your reputation and (hopefully) your pride and second, an unrivaled opportunity to win that customer's loyalty for a long time to come. Scurry to do everything possible to bat two for two by restoring the first and securing the second. Nothing else makes any sense at all to me. The necessary processes and the constant monitoring of response effectiveness must be championed from the highest level of the business. My universal law is: If a customer has one genuine grievance, do two things to solve it.

Is all this TOR stuff really worth the bother? Why should we care about them? After all, they are not about technical competitiveness or marketplace distinction. All of us see examples of businesspeople and activities that blatantly ignore TOR but that "succeed" anyway, and I guess some role models achieve their cult status not just by ignoring TOR but by openly doing the opposite. Can the best case we make for them only be structured around conscience and feel-good factors?

Increasing evidence points in a different direction, suggesting that the right corporate behavior contributes to a competitive advantage and that the negative consequences of doing wrong things are profound. The Walker Group's research unit (Walker Research) surveyed a nationally representative sample of U.S. households in 1994, seeking trends in customer propensity to respond to business practices, community treatment, employee treatment, and environmental responsibilities when making their purchasing decisions. Forty-seven percent indicated they would be much more likely to buy from "good" companies, but I was much more interested in the implications for the bad guys: Fifty-seven percent indicated they would *avoid* buying products from an organization that used questionable business practices. The key to the door here might not be to accentuate the positive, but to highlight the potential downside of the negative. A similar result came from a survey of investors, 39 percent of whom said they frequently check on the business practices and values of a company before investing.

All forward progress in capitalism derives from the pursuit of a vested self-interest. If there is evidence that you can take some cash to the bank (or more likely, avoid losing cash) by doing a few things right, then that is encouraging. But it's not what I want to base my case for my TOR on. I do not believe you have to abandon the basic graces and integrities of ascended humanity to succeed in business, nor do I believe it is a new-fangled, quasi-liberal idea to think that way. A number of my TOR simply suggest that you treat others in your circle of business acquaintance as if they were of your own blood. As early as the 1920s Konosuke Matsushita insisted that you should "Treat the people you do business with as if they were part of your family." He, of course, founded the mighty Panasonic. In case you rush to the conclusion that he was a liberal softie, treading water in some unprofitable love-in, he also had a few words on wealth creation: "If we cannot make a profit, that means we are committing a sort of crime against society."

The pressures at all levels of business to ignore or break the tests of rightness are immense. I should know. Although I cannot remember truly abusing a boss–subordinate relationship from above, I've left most of the other TORs in bits many times. Most of the time I knew immediately or soon afterward, and I was daft enough to try to fix them as soon as the penny dropped. I was not driven by the profit implications or Japanese wisdom, but simply by a feeling of what was sensible and civilized behavior. There are times when it is right to fight a battle even when perceived wisdom discourages you and there is a real chance you will lose the war. As Churchill said, "Never give in. Never, never, never give in, except to convictions of honor and good sense." The revisionists have cast a lot of clouds over the guy, but that approach still works for me.

Riding home from work tonight, look back on your day. Apply TOR to your main activities—everything from decisions you've made to the way you've acted. Think about it, away from the workplace, in the decompression chamber leading to your other life where you deal with people, spend your money, and behave oh-so-differently. For some reason....

If something you've done suddenly doesn't feel right, turn the car around or stop the train. Fix it before you go to bed. This stuff's important. In the long run it will define what you stand for in business, and that is far more important than achieving today's batch of downsizing goals or actually making money from a computer upgrade.

Sadly, Barbara Tuchman died in February 1989, and I am left with the task of ranking the great mistakes of the 1990s in her overall list of history's greatest. There have, of course, been a number of them. In the business world we saw the doomed launch of New Coke and in the exciting world of science we witnessed the British sheep-cloning project.[13] Princess Fergie qualifies as a mistake in her own right, naturally, while the world of sport gave us Mike Tyson's ear-biting escapades. Saddam Hussein has a chapter all to himself. After a lot of thought, however, I've recorded only one mistake as deserving of inclusion

---

[13]I visit England a lot. Last time I drove any distance across the country, the one thing that didn't strike me was a need for more sheep.

on the list of all-time greats. I refer, of course, to Hugh Grant's trouserless escapade with a hooker in his BMW. I have ranked him above Montezuma (for greeting the Spanish invasion pleasantly instead of fighting, and thus losing Mexico) but below Rehoboam, son of King Solomon, who, by failing all of the TOR we've listed above and many more that he invented himself, lost the ten northern tribes of his father's kingdom, collectively called Israel.

Now that's what I call being in good company.

# 2

# On Motivational Theory

A long time ago, probably before Albert Dunlap had fired his first nanny,[1] I attended one of England's most prestigious post-grad business schools. It was beautifully situated along the upper reaches of the River Thames, and I spent many long hours in the nineteenth-century library learning how to spell the words *paradigm* and *osmosis*. Without those words, of course, I would never have become a Captain of Industry.

Lectures came and went as I meandered amiably toward my master's degree. In truth, I found very little of what I learned was relevant when I finally went into the locker room of corporate management. Don't get me wrong: I recorded some notable triumphs during my time at the school. The highlight, I believe, was the consumption of a remarkable thirty-four glasses of slivova (a rather primitive plum brandy) during one sitting while on an exchange visit to the Karl Marx Institute of Economics in Sofia, Bulgaria. This was well before the fall of Communism and occurred during a debate with a local student on the hot-button topic of whether Neil Young had played with the Flying Burrito Brothers.

---

[1]Just after he did this he actually sold the remaining family.

Obviously I do not remember the details, but I understand my consumption still stands as a national all-comers record, despite the visit of Boris Yeltsin some years later.

My master's degree was also notable for being my third business qualification, all of which had accounting in them somewhere, in which I never got a trial balance to do so. It was at this stage of my career that I made the decision not to join Coopers and Lybrand.

I have only one other memory of business school, the lecture we heard on motivational theory. Out came the Gospel According to Maslow and Hertzberg, seminal works on the subject opining that a man (this was the 1970s; women in business hadn't been invented yet) required more out of his work than just cash. In fact the cash bit was usually achieved quite quickly and a whole bunch of other needs suddenly appeared on the radar screen, including, in no particular order (and probably incomplete because I'm working from memory): job satisfaction, job enrichment, empowerment, responsibility, somebody to talk and listen to, recognition, and so on blahblahblahblah.... Students memorized the key words *hygiene factors* and *hierarchy of needs* and whacked them into every conceivable essay in the pursuit of a guaranteed additional five marks. I'm not just talking about business essays here; I know I inserted them in an essay on wheat farming in Canada and scored well.

I was unhappy with these ideas, but really too bored to think them through and suggest alternatives. In fact I was more than bored. My ingoing position on their theories (please remember, this flame was fanned by the arrogance of youth) was that I could probably eat a couple of cans of Alphabetti-Spaghetti and defecate better ideas on the subject. But I let it rest. I felt the theories would never be appropriate in business, and they never were. I presumed they'd ended up with Keynes' multiplier in some mystic dumpster for guru thoughts that had passed their shelf life, shortly to be joined by the arrival of trickle-down economics.

Not so. Recently I did some work with the University of Miami's Business School, a fine program headed by an energetic and forward-thinking dean and populated by capable, tenured[2]

---

[2]Has there ever been a dafter idea? Possibly synchronized swimming?

professors who floss their teeth and publish papers and so on. Astonishingly this crap is still on the menu, and I was forced to try to figure some things out, maybe twenty years too late to be of any use.

Let's try to pick up some ideas about what makes folks enthusiastic (a.k.a. motivates them):

◆ I'll start by looking in my mirror. I left big business a few years ago, for good. Despite the absence of Tiger Woods' agent and any deal with Nike, I negotiated an exit deal with my corporation that enabled me to choose to leave and that parachuted more money into my bank account than I'd ever dreamed of owning. I am not richer than God, but if you adjust for inflation, I am probably more liquid than he was when he was fifty. Based on our current lifestyle, my wife and I have enough cash to last us 3981 years. But what was the first thing I did when I was free? *I sat down to figure out how I could earn more.*

◆ Let's now take a well-to-do family earning well above the national average income. Let's even take it toward the extreme and say two or three times that level, presumably well above the "monetarily satisfied" level defined by Messrs. Hertzberg and Maslow. Let's have a closer look at this family, which is probably at just about breakeven after taxes, mortgage (maybe two of those), credit card debt service, car loans or leases, school fees, health insurance, plus the cosmetic stuff you have to acquire when you're nearly rich to prove to yourself and your neighbors that you're actually rich. All this comes before the family provides for future liabilities for college tuition (now officially estimated at $2 million per year per student by the year 2010; at least that's what the projection is for the University of Miami), retirement (for which, by my estimation, you need a lump sum of $15 million[3]), aging parents, and so on and so on.

Now, try telling these "elite" folks they've got enough money and should now concentrate only on feel-good stuff.

◆ Now we change tack to one of my rare true stories. A business I know in multi- (small) unit retailing was grappling with the eternal problem of getting the right people to do the right

[3]This excludes any dental work you may need.

things at store level, a challenge made even more difficult by the fact the outlets were kiosks, with few staff operating for long, unattractive hours. The central management team was exploring the idea of abandoning the traditional span-breaking district manager supervising six or so units and instead promoting one of the unit managers into a team-leading role. He or she would still run a unit, albeit with more staff, but would take on the added responsibility of managing two or three other units. It was thought that this plan would bring more cohesion, commitment, and responsibility to a smaller group, nearer the customer. Good thinking. Everything's okay so far.

They planned to sell this idea to the projected prototype team leader (a female) with the sound logic that she should welcome the added responsibility, see it as recognition, and be really excited about the obvious signal that she had been earmarked for future growth. At this stage, they decided there would be no other compensation needed. They were amazed when she told them to pound sand and left the company the following Wednesday. (Author's note: I did not personally know the woman, but I was very proud of her).

◆ Now we head off to Switzerland for the last point on this rather odd scattergraph:

Some years ago, while working for GrandMet, I was part of a team that acquired a small chain of pasta restaurants based in Lucerne. The quality of service was legendary and a clear market differentiator. I asked the founder-entrepreneur how he got his folks so fired up. He looked at me as though I was stupid and, as it turns out, on this subject, I was.

Each month he simply paid the restaurant team the collective Swiss minimum wage or a pool of cash equivalent to 20 percent of sales—*whichever was the highest.*[4] Once a month he'd get them all around a big table and, expressing concerns about the service levels, threaten to add another staff person. The staff, of course, saw this as another mouth to feed from their reward pool, so service became even more spectacular. He never recruited the additional person and he never paid out the minimum wage.

[4]Or some similar percentage, I can't remember exactly. The figure is not important, so go back to the script and catch the *principle.*

But other forces were at work as well. The staff realized that a repeat visit by a customer would help next month's salary pool as well, so they worked at building relationships, with the goal of bringing people back for repeat purchases. Before somebody yells about exploitation of labor or piece-rate slavery, let me tell you that the spirit in the place was fabulous. They got the highest tips in the city and had the lowest staff turnover I've seen in nearly thirty years associated with service retailing. Whenever a job vacancy arose, the number of applicants was overwhelming.

We've had four little vignettes to digest and we are now ready for Gibbons' two universal laws of motivation.

**Universal Law #10**

*People are coin operated. Period. Understand that and do not patronize them.*

First: People are coin operated. Period. Understand that, and do not patronize them. If you are an enlightened capitalist you will meet their other needs, in the interests of both the company and the individual, but it's not *after* the cash or *instead* of it, it's *as well as*. If you are going to mix it all up, a good rule of thumb is ten parts cash for every one part of feel-good.

**Universal Law #11**

*Share the rewards from any corporate gain with those who gained it.*

Second: When you are faced with a corporate problem and you analyze it to death behind your closed boardroom door and shape a proposed solution, *think carefully* about what you'll do next. If you implement the solution and the company reaps the gains but those who do the actual implementing get nothing but supposedly feel-good stuff, you are likely (and here we will use advanced motivational theory terminology) to pee all over your own shoes. We are talking about making people enthusiastic, and a good starting point is not to get them to do it for you, have the investors pocket any gain, and give them no share. The way to get a second strike against you is to then tell employees you really do believe that they have just climbed their own hierarchy of needs.

One of the core paradoxes mentioned in the introduction to this book concerns motivation: At a time when we need motivated and savvy people we have the most alienated workforces in history. Most people understand that they are employed on sufferance and that if the company could do without them it would. From the other side, employees have little or no loyalty toward the corporation, although relationships with individual mentors, bosses, or teammates can be magnetic. Professors are more likely to feel affinity with fellow academics working in the same field but in other universities than with their own colleges. This development has been catalyzed by the Web and E-mail and, in time, will affect all peer group and loyalty structures. The science of corporate employment is becoming similar to what flourished in the old Wild West: hiring gunslingers for the protection or development of your interests. When the job is done, a fistful of dollars is paid and everyone moves on.

Other than by giving lots of dollars and a share of any gain, formal efforts to motivate people have become irrelevant to modern business life. I do see a lot of factors at work that contribute, sometimes unconsciously or indirectly, to an employee's ability or willingness to contribute fully. Downsizing is a fine example of this, and I am not talking about the implications for the poor bastards given the pink slip; it is the "survivors" that concern me here. Downsizing is normally driven by the desire to cut costs, but it does no such thing in its own right. Getting rid of people does not cut costs, the same way that cutting budgets does not cut costs. *Only cutting costs cuts costs.* What frequently happens is that people are fired and budgets are cut, but the work that

**Universal Law #12**
*Getting rid of people does not cut costs, the same way that cutting budgets does not cut costs.* Only cutting costs cuts costs.

needs doing stays the same and has to be outsourced (expensively) or spread among the folks who remain (a factor largely responsible for the advent of the mandatory long working week and a ton of tension and alienation). I am convinced that we need to spend less time on sophisticated theories of motivation and a lot more time on simple ways to avoid de-motivation. In my book, the management of the working week is a good place to start.

True story: I attended a charity lunch recently and shared a table with one of H. Wayne Huizenga's[5] right-hand guys. We quickly found we had one thing in common: a wish that we could have just written a check to the charity and not had to receive in return the benefit of an appalling meal and a gaggle of excruciating speakers. We chatted quietly between ourselves to pass the time.

He was a real nice guy.[6] Responding to a polite inquiry from him, I told him what I'd been doing over the last couple of days, revealing what I suppose has become a business routine since my retirement as a Captain of Industry.

◆ I get up when our youngest dog (Scuddy[7]) threatens to finally break the bedroom door down. The time varies depending on whether he (the dog) has had a late night.

◆ I meander around the kitchen assembling coffee, and debate (with myself) whether there is any way I can justify going out for a bagel after a heavy dinner the previous evening. I decide, emphatically, that this must be a work day.

◆ ...DaDaaahhhh! I switch my computer on. I quickly pass through the decompression chamber that leads me from the real world into a virtual universe of communication, data

[5]He of sequential empires in waste management, videos (Blockbuster), automobiles (AutoNation), and most of Florida's sports franchises. His exit from Blockbuster will go down in history as one of the great examples of selling at the top.

[6]I hope this statement doesn't get him fired.

[7]Named after the Scud missile that the world got to know in the Gulf War. It's the one that sets off with an objective in mind but rapidly forgets it and flips about all over the place. Mostly harmless. Reminds me a lot of Steve Jobs.

banks, interactivity, analysis, and my English soccer team's home page. Lost again.

♦ Enough soccer. Into Personal Finance to get last night's stock closing price on a company I've invested in. Down a quarter and somebody dumped several thousand shares. I shout "Bastards" at the screen, in a voice loud enough to make our eldest dog (Joss[8]) jump out of his skin.

♦ Turn off the computer. Enough of that. Amble over to the fax and find an overnight note from the CEO of a California start-up company (of which I am chairman) informing me that we've run out of cash. Again. I fax him back, telling him to instruct our broker-bankers to switch the search for investors away from IFF sources (i.e., Immediate Family and Friends) and to seek what is universally known in the investment world as TFD[9] finance.

♦ Now it's time to work out. I slip into my Nike form-fitting shorts and my Air Gibbons sneakers, and lie down on the bedroom floor. I carefully divide all my wife's credit cards into two piles, balance one pile in each hand, and then raise them to the full extension of my arm. I repeat this five times.

♦ By the time I shower, it's time for my power nap. I was introduced to this concept by a New York securities dealer who worked for Nomura.[10] He would leave the trading floor at 1:30 P.M. precisely each day (true story), go to his cubicle, unhook his suspenders, and sleep for three minutes. He insisted this sharpened him for the pre-close session on Wall Street. My power nap lasts an hour and a quarter.

---

[8]Named after the Chinese house god if you are interested. I didn't think you were....

[9]Two F---ing Dentists (a widespread source of start-up capital for U.S. businesses).

[10]Believe it or not, I had been invited to give a motivational speech to the traders. I was sandwiched between two internal speakers, one of whom had just received a $9 million bonus, and the other $4.5 million. The average bonus received by members of the audience was in seven figures. My theory was proven: These folks did not need motivating. So I told some jokes.

- At dinnertime I summon up a mixture of courage and grace, approach my wife, and suggest that she take a rest from cooking and that we go out for supper. She grimaces, and there is a long pause before she utters a reluctant: "Well...okay. But just this once." For the record, this is the 435th consecutive evening that this exact conversation has taken place.

- Finally to bed, having surfed late-night TV in vain for anything with Chuck Norris in it.

By now my new Huizenga buddy[11] was dozing quietly, so I woke him and inquired about *his* last couple of days. (Author's note: I've never been one for overresearching my work and I can't remember which part of Wayne's world this guy was from. The following probably narrows it down to about ten or fifteen people.)

His story was astonishing. In one day, starting at 3:30 A.M. in Fort Lauderdale in a private plane, he had hit Los Angeles, Montreal, and Boston and got back to south Florida. The preceding day (and about 1000 such days) involved the same sort of thing, and another trip was planned for the next day (and about another 1000). My companion had fifty to eighty live acquisition projects in his briefcase at any given time. That's the way of life when you work closely with Wayne, and it's not optional. I know many more like this guy, in many other companies—and so do you.

Until a couple of years ago that was my life. Long, long days, endless travel, waking up in strange hotel rooms, checking the language on the bedside phone instructions to remember what country I was in, days of meetings from breakfast through dinner. Missing our sons growing inches I would never see again. Always running late, behind on returning phone calls, and not taking enough time for *anybody* in my business or personal worlds.

Yup, you're right. I was paid a ton of cash for this angst, and I guess the guy from Wayne's world is more than a heart-

---

[11] Remember him?

beat away from welfare. And, yup, you're right again: Both he and I had a choice. If we didn't like it we could quit, and I'll make no bones about it: Leaving that crap behind was a factor in my decision to do so.

I believe the advent of the repeated seventy-hour week is a core business problem today, but it's not about me or my new-found buddy. Do not feel sorry for the elite, the top one percent who, because of the salary levels they enjoy, have profoundly more money than sense and financial safety nets that enable them to walk away and do something else.

The real issue emerges when the extended workweek hits the masses, the bulk of the management and staff that make up most corporations. Over the last decade or two, far from the predicted world of increased leisure, the workweek has expand-ed, in some cases dramatically, for the ordinary man and woman. Reengineering (common definition: doing the same tasks with dramatically fewer people), cost cutting (usually including recruitment and replacement freezes), and misguided investments in systems and technology (that do not deliver the planned savings in staff hours, but staff are fired anyway) have all led to crisis-level underresourcing in many corporations.

Of course, the only option *not* available to management in these cases is to 'fess up. Stop and think whether you have ever heard, or even heard, of a manager of any profile or signif-icance addressing an analyst's meeting or an employee group, and opening with these words: "Er...well...er, well...look, we put this ball in the rough. That reengineering/downsizing/cost cut-ting/huge investment in technology [delete as applicable] ...er, well,...it didn't come through as planned and we're taking those 11,000 folks back on. If they'll have us."

No. The only variable left to tweak is the working week of the remaining employees, which is mostly adjusted (upward) without incremental compensation. A U.S. Labor Department study published in the fall of 1998 recorded a 22 percent jump in the length of the average workday in the U.S. private sector over the last decade (from 8 hours to 9.6). A lot of this isn't vol-untary or even welcome. When a bunch of folks looks really closely at their employment contracts, they find a mandatory overtime element.

Sure, these folks have a choice; but telling your employer to stick his or her job where the sun don't shine is nervy (to say the least) in a world where the number of jobs needing yesterday's skills is in irrevocable decline.

I wish I had a buck for everyone in business who ever felt trapped like this. But the amazing fact is that there are folks in this predicament *who you should not feel sorry for.* These folks *celebrate* this crap. This is usually a male thing, and it is partly due to the perception that long weeks are "expected" and it's "the way it is today." But only partly. Another part is due to a sort of weird "glee" factor—that this guy, some twenty years after he last wore athletic shorts, is in such demand and can still physically perform with the best of them. Somehow this morphs into an overt test of masculinity. It is important to prove this to his family, his peers, his subordinates, and the reflection in his own shaving mirror. It is truly one of the few recognized, overt, and widely franchised virility contests left in the world.

Is there a sensible approach to handling this in business today?[12] The two keys are *individuality* and *sustainability.*

I can go ninety hours a week with the best of them, and I know business sometimes demands it. This isn't always tied to money or compensation. I've done this throughout my life since I joined Shell as a clerk thirty years ago on a weekly salary roughly the inflation-adjusted equivalent of the price of today's Burger King value meal. I can do two of these weeks if needed, possibly three, and maybe stretch it to a fourth. Then it gets counterproductive, 'cos I'm out of gas. It takes me twice the time to figure anything out and my error rate doubles; that's my own *corporate biorhythm.* Others

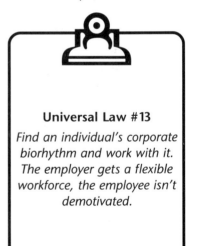

**Universal Law #13**

*Find an individual's corporate biorhythm and work with it. The employer gets a flexible workforce, the employee isn't demotivated.*

---

[12]The challenge of continuous seventy-hour weeks, not virility contests.

flag after one long week, others never seem to (Margaret Thatcher is rumored to have slept an average of only four hours a night for the thirteen years she was in power—a figure that is interpreted by many different people in many different ways). The enlightened employer, who makes decisions as to how best to allocate resources during a short-term crisis in the smallest groups at the nearest possible point to the crisis, knows the individual biorhythms of the team members and uses them to create the flexibility needed.

We move on from managing a short-term emergency to addressing a sustainable resource demand that seems to require permanent long workweeks from everybody just to get by. This is not rocket science, and my own rule of thumb is that is if you expect (i.e., it is an unwritten, implicit part of the contract of employment) all your folks to work more than fifty hours a week for more than an emergency two or three weeks, then you are building your business on a San Andreas fault. It could implode at any time. The message is simple: You need more people. You are lying to yourself, your people, and your investors if you ignore that fact. Moreover, you will not sustain the quality of your product or service and understaffing will cost you money sooner rather than later.

**Universal Law #14**

*Responding to a short-term crisis is one thing, but a company that tries to sustain business with employees consistently working more than fifty hours a week is built on a San Andreas fault.*

Remember, working long hours does not mean necessarily mean working smart. Activity does not automatically yield effectiveness. You need smart and effective people to win battles in the marketplace, not folks who turn up for long periods of time and do stuff.[13] If you get this wrong, you get demotivated, alienated people.[14]

[13]E.g., the French Government.

[14]At this point I apologize to my many women readers for concentrating much of this diatribe on males. There are two reasons for that: First, I am convinced we (males) are a big part of the problem and second, I cannot come up with a female equivalent of a virility contest.

It would be wrong not to acknowledge some of the New Wave approaches to motivation, which usually involve some little (cheap) concessions that make the workplace a kinder, gentler environment. Bring Your Daughter to Work Day is one such jewel, but the best of them is built around the revolutionary concept that wearing a polo shirt in the office for one day a week will turn you into some sort of corporate world-beater. Dress Down Friday has arrived....

It has been some time since I trotted away from my position as the unchallenged thoroughbred in Calvin Klein's stable of male models. A rigid diet consisting only of lavender-scented cigarettes and Calvados positioned me at the vanguard of the angular, waiflike look so revered in the world of high fashion, but I felt it was time to move on. Also, being head of Burger King jeopardized my image somewhat, heralding as it did the advent of some inappropriate extra chins.[15] I have, however, kept in touch with the mercurial world of men's business fashion and have observed the coming of Dress Down Friday with delight.

Dress Down Friday is the practice of some corporations to tolerate replacing the normal business uniform with attire defined as *business casual*. Normal uniform for the male, of course, is defined as jacket and pants of the same dark material (with the elbows shining like Greta Garbo's eyes), sensible shoes (cleaned every time you pass through the airport), a conservative shirt, a dark tie, and a minimum of exposed jewelry unless you work in Miami. The sole exception to the latter rule applies when you reach senior management, when it becomes mandatory to sport a Rolex watch the size of an ice hockey puck.

Business casual now takes the place of all this, sometimes for the whole of Friday each week.[16] We live in enlightened times.

The Dress Down Friday movement is demand driven, or at least that's what the suits in the boardroom believe. It is an attempt to address one of the core big business paradoxes of our times: When companies desperately need the shrunk-

[15]Three at the last count.

[16]Whoop, as they say, pee.

en, pressurized residue of people that make up their workforce to be enthusiastic and motivated, they continue to treat 'em like dog poop. This, of course, makes them unenthusiastic and demotivated.

This paradox takes up a lot of board time because it's difficult to find appropriate bones to throw to the dogs to reverse the effect. The basic rule is simple—it's got to make 'em feel good *but not cost anything*—and the company's Vice President of Tokenism is usually charged with developing a series of options for the board to discuss. The subject is usually debated after lunch, between proposals for next year's Strategic Board Retreat in Rio and drawing straws to decide who's going to champion the company's next United Way campaign.

After a painful board process and several Human Resource papers on the subject (e.g., An Executive Guide to Business Casual: Avoiding the Paradigm Shift), the CEO announces the new policy to the adoring masses. If the CEO is a guy, this is done with unbridled locker-room enthusiasm, a technique picked up at a recent interpersonal skills and diversity workshop. He then, of course, proceeds to lead by personal example.

To the workforce, which has been enormously entertained so far, this development is just hilarious. The CEO is clearly beached: He knows everyone will be watching him next Friday, but he has absolutely no idea what to wear (and if he had there would be nothing in his closet that would be remotely appropriate). So he rubs the Only in America genie lamp and out pops the Personal Wardrobe Advisor, whose job is to take such weight and responsibility from the CEO's poor, burdened shoulders. The result? The following Friday the lower ranks are greeted by the sight of the CEO wearing the sort of outfit that Prince Charles has one of his valets select for a post–polo match ambassador's reception. The loafers alone cost $1200.

The folks grin among themselves, bets are settled, and life goes on. The local discount store does a sudden roaring trade in imperfect designer polo shirts, and Dress Down Friday has arrived.

Not many CEOs have the benefit of having their corporate headquarters (together with the homes of more than half the employees) obliterated by a hurricane. For those who haven't, *benefit* may seem to be an odd choice of word. I admit that none of us involved felt life was being overly kind to us when Hurricane Andrew wiped out Burger King's corporate HQ and thousands of homes in the immediate vicinity in 1992.

It is only with hindsight and with everybody's workplace, homes, and lives back in order again that I can see the gains we made from this trauma. Some were truly personal, like the fact that the $20,000 grotesque orange leather sofa that one of my predecessors imported from Italy (and that I couldn't bring myself to throw away because it had cost so much) ended up somewhere in Texas.[17] Some benefits were essentially corporate, such as the fact we lost about 7000 filing cabinets stuffed with crap we'd been storing for years simply because our lawyers told us we had to. It turns out we didn't have to, and we know that now because the stuff is at the bottom of the Gulf of Mexico and we don't miss it.

So it was with clothes. Just before the hurricane hit we had two board papers ready for discussion, a proposal to introduce Dress Down Friday and another for experimenting with limited flextime. When we reassembled just after the storm in a temporary building, wearing whatever we had left and in between trying to find roofers to secure our homes, we realized how comical those proposals were in the light of what we were facing.

There was no alternative. Good artists copy, great artists steal. We stole Nordstrom's legendary one-line operations manual and applied it to both our dress code and flextime: *At all times use your own best judgment.* There would be no dress code, and work hours would be sorted out and agreed to team by team. People were challenged (enabled? empowered? *trusted?*) to figure it out for themselves.

The results were so glorious that very quickly we followed up by telling everyone policies on either dress code or flextime would only be reinstated if the teams demonstrated they were unable to continue managing themselves. A year later,

[17]I repeat, it was *orange*. What they dyed the leather with I will never know, but my respect for the Italian nation grew when I saw it.

**41**

when we got back in our HQ and life got back to something near normal, the teams were still in charge.

Anybody surprised out there? Lots of raised eyebrows? So was I and so were mine. That response highlights one of the core problems in business today. The results we got were nothing more than you would expect if you asked a bunch of responsible people to manage themselves. Why does it seem to take a hurricane or some such crisis to get us to try the idea out? People used excellent judgement. If there was a need to visit or be visited by an external party, they respected the event and dressed conservatively. Nobody abused it for long, and we didn't need anyone to police the policy. Peers used the wonderful chemistry and processes that only peers can. The surprise is only that we are surprised.

To many I am a dress renegade, accused of being a maverick without respect for the traditions of business, of which dress and appearance have been an important part since the Armani codpiece was introduced to an astounded Venetian Rialto a few centuries back. Maybe. I don't think the dress debate should be about uniformity and conservatism. It should be about personal judgement, standards, and tastes (JSTs) and if the end results for you are such that you want to look like everybody who's ever worked for IBM, that's fine by me. But it would be nice if you showed the same tolerance for my JSTs.

I shared nearly fifty years on this earth with my father, who spent the years up to and including the Second World War as a regular army officer and during my adolescent years served in local government. His dress was conservative and uniform, understandable given his background. He dressed that way partly because that's what he knew and partly because his JSTs were impeccable. I'm pretty sure I never saw him unshaven, and very rarely without a necktie. As a consequence we had many arm wrestles about my own JSTs (or perceived lack of them). Remember, I believed profoundly that Elvis was some sort of second coming and that the wearing of blue jeans tripled my sexual magnetism.[18]

[18]Turns out I was right about the latter, but the bad news is that the whole thing took place on a very low mathematical scale.

Dad's influence stayed with me in that I developed my own JSTs, and managed to survive and thrive in three relatively conservative large businesses. My closet contained dark suits and if I had doubts about an occasion I chose to err on the side of sobriety. There were times, however, when I was working solo or with peers in an informal setting and was frequently mistaken for a panhandler. Indeed, Kurt Cobain is rumored to have studied a photo of my appearance at a 1989 cultural diversity workshop to develop his rather thoughtful grunge look. But most of the time I pitched it somewhere in between and managed to avoid arrest.

When it comes to dress codes, as in the vast majority of all business challenges, the universal rule is simple: Spend time hiring the right people and then let go. Folks know what to do. The bad news is they probably have a better feel for what's appropriate than the suits in the boardroom, who lost touch with the real world the first time they flew in a private jet. Let the ordinary folk use their own JSTs, and the world (and your business) will be a better place. Just don't make a big deal out of it, okay?

My summary universal law on motivation is: Pay people till their eyes water, give them a share of the value they add, trust them, and avoid doing stupid things to de-motivate them. It will be howled down, I'm sure. The international HR militia, from their HQ in the Blue Ridge Mountains, will probably issue a fatwa against me and business psychologists will argue that motivation is far more complicated than I make out. But

**Universal Law #15**

*Dress codes are dumb. Spend time hiring the right people and then just let go. They know how to dress. Oh, and when you do let go, don't make a big deal out of it, okay?*

**Universal Law #16**

*Summary universal law of motivation: Pay people till their eyes water, share with them the value they add, trust them, and avoid doing dumb things that de-motivate them.*

when I look back on the successes I've been associated with, I realize they've usually been achieved by a bunch of people who would go through steel doors for me. It ain't complicated. Getting seven and a half million transistors on a computer chip strikes me as complicated; motivating people doesn't. Motivation takes time and thought and a willingness to share gains. Which is why, I guess, a lot of people figure it is complicated.

# On Enlightened Capitalism (or Should That Be Enlightened Capitalists?)

Many people believe that the optimal political model is a Singapore-style benign dictatorship, but I am not among them. Similarly, many believe that enlightened capitalism is the best economic model, and I share that belief. The problem with both concepts is that my definitions of them probably (make that *certainly*) differ from yours. Both concepts are based on interpreting "bits" of this factor and "bits" of that element and often seem to apply to a set of particular circumstances that make them difficult to transfer. They are also like the Intel chip: Millions of people have heard about it, but if somebody put one on a table right in front of you, you wouldn't recognize it for what it was.[1]

Is enlightened capitalism about employees who can't wait to get to work? High investor returns? Effective and efficient operations or service? Great products? Being environmentally responsible? Not treating your vendors like dog poop?

---

[1]I would have the same trouble with a female contraceptive and the rock band Pearl Jam.

Avoiding but not evading taxes? Having a clear vision? Demonstrating impeccable ethics? Acting with political correctness? Or all of the above?

As with many things, the best way to pin it down is to rule out what it isn't. Sherlock Holmes made us face the self-evident: When everything else has been ruled out, whatever's left, however unlikely, must be the answer.[2]

We are immediately aware that enlightened capitalism cannot be just one-dimensional, which, to my delight, rules out some oft-toted examples like Ben and Jerry's (ice cream) and The Body Shop (personal care products) as the perfect role models. Both companies claim the high ground from an environmentally friendly point of view[3], and both have some justification for so doing. They both use this position as a charter for corporate culture as well as for market distinction. I am also a personal fan of Anita Roddick's gutsy approach to business, as evidenced by the way she overcame barrier after barrier during the genesis of The Body Shop. But both brands in my view are competitive underperformers, and champions (of any kind) don't underperform.

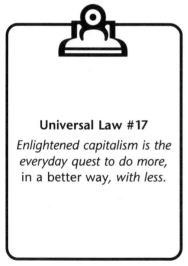

**Universal Law #17**
*Enlightened capitalism is the everyday quest to do more, in a better way, with less.*

It is an age-old management axiom that the daily challenge of business is to do more, do it better, and with less. With a bit of tinkering that may lead us to a starting position for our universal laws of enlightened capitalism. We just change the middle bit and it becomes doing more, *in a better way*, with less. This moves it on from just continually making your product and services better and starts to include *how* you do things as well as *what* you do. This makes the challenge much more difficult and our champions much harder to find.

We should pause here to see if we can untangle the capitalist factor from capitalism. Big corpora-

---

[2]This law has governed my career. I am still ruling things out to see what's left.

[3]Just beating out Union Carbide for their contribution at Bhopal, India.

tions, certainly in the West, are often led by big personalities, and the culture and style of the business somehow becomes inextricably linked with the person. Phil Knight (Nike), Michael Eisner (Disney), Tony O'Reilly (Heinz), Roberto Goizuetta (Coca-Cola), Jack Welch (GE), Bill Gates (Microsoft), Ted Turner, Rupert Murdoch, Lee Iacocca, James Goldsmith, Andy Groves....That is a profoundly incomplete list of examples of business leaders whose personalities seem to be reflected in the way their companies approach (or approached) their business. If we put "do more...with less" on the back burner for a while, and concentrate on the "in a better way" part, we begin to digest the fact that although technical skills remain important, the style, spirit, values, and personality of the leadership of the business (not necessarily only that of the Big Cheese but heavily influenced by him or her) grow in the mix.

Again, we can start to get a clearer picture by agreeing what enlightened capitalism isn't, and here I am going to begin by apologizing to Al Franken, that fine comedian and writer, and slightly amending his book title that referred specifically to the loopy right-wing radio journalist Rush Limbaugh. My version is: *Al Dunlap is a big fat idiot.*[4]

At first sight, Mr. Dunlap seems a strange place to start this particularly negative journey. Prior to his hilarious sacking by Sunbeam, he had been enormously successful and is a (self-confessed) icon of wealth creation. At the Scott Paper Company he savagely improved stockholder returns—and I do mean savagely. On his appointment to beleaguered Sunbeam, before he'd even put his foot in the door, the stock value went through the roof. Portfolio managers began tracking Albert on his way to work, on the basis that if his car *drove past* the HQ of one of their investment companies it would hike the stock price a few points.

So what's my beef with the guy? Have I no respect for somebody able enough to create massive improvements in stockholder wealth wherever he's paused for a month or two on his journey to immortality? A journey which, as a byproduct, created hundreds of millions of dollars of wealth for himself.

---

[4]I apologize. This is wrong and I know it. Mr. Dunlap is *not* a big fat idiot. I have seen a photograph of him and he is more of a medium-sized, quite slim idiot. Sorry.

Of course I have respect for him, but it's the same bizarre respect I hold for O. J. Simpson (for having sullied the jury system that has delivered justice for much of the Western world for the best part of a millennium[5]); for Saddam Hussein (who took a TKO in the Gulf War, then carried on as though nothing had happened); and for Don King (for some reason, which is quite beyond my comprehension, boxing works *because* of Don King, not *despite* him). Yup, you gotta admire these folks.

Don't get me wrong here; Dunlap's logic and tactics are sound. Faced with certain death, many would choose survival as a multiple amputee, which is what he offers. In the world of medicine the specialist amputation surgeon has an honorable role to play. But that is not what medicine is about. The real heroes are the folks who work their butts off preventing the vast, vast majority of the human race from becoming critically ill. Similarly, in the wonderful world of wealth creation, the real heroes are the enlightened capitalists who dedicate themselves (again, often unheralded) to keeping their companies healthy and far from a state in which (to mix a few metaphors) some Narcissus can drift in and get rich and famous by plucking some low-hanging fruit.

I've got a real beef with Al Dunlap—two, in fact. The first is a style thing, which is so important in shaping *how* things get done in a business. Keep an airline sick bag handy and read Dunlap's book[6] or at least get as far as I did, which was almost to the end of page one. Note that on the first page of text, actually only about two-thirds of a full page, the word *I* appears thirteen times, a figure that leads me to believe (as we get onto full pages and his enthusiasm for the subject increases) that the book will have about 3500 such references. Ugh.

I don't have a huge problem with self-publicity. I grin and shrug my shoulders with the rest of you when Princess Fergie's latest controlled photo opportunity hits the media or when Charlie Sheen does something outrageous to combat falling box

---

[5]This does betray my hitherto unpublished view on O. J. Simpson: The only difference between O. J. and (say) Hitler was that Hitler actually left fewer clues.

[6]*Mean Business*, with Bob Andelman (Random House, 1996).

office receipts. In sport or entertainment this behavior is fair game because it reflects an individual trying to optimize the business of his or her unique talent. What you see is what you get—literally, the individual. But in business, the superstars are different. They head organizations that reflect the skills and commitments of thousands of people and a variety of stakeholders.

It's so easy to fall into the show-biz trap. Keep that sick bag handy and read the following:

> In 1989 I joined Burger King Corporation—a company that had lost its way. No growth, no profitability, a shattered quality ethic, bruised franchisee relationships, thirteen layers of management,[7] and an international business in tatters. I left in 1994, by which time I had increased profitability, expanded the company to fifty countries, achieved a growth rate of 500 to 600 restaurants a year, introduced rigid quality control, and reduced layers of management to five. I had also introduced Disney and Coca-Cola as strategic marketing partners, developed a range of relevant new products, reengineered the supply chain, and navigated the business through a hurricane that destroyed its HQ and the homes of half its central management and staff.

What you have there is history à la Dunlap, and several cubic feet of flatulence. Of course I was there, and proud to be Chairman and CEO; and of course I had a role to play, and an important one at that. But the results we achieved were due to a bunch of management and staff doing their thing while under the stress of constant uncertainty; and a bunch of vendors continuing to invest in production improvements because they believed in the system; and franchisees building restaurants with dark clouds

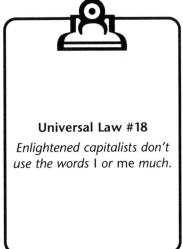

**Universal Law #18**

*Enlightened capitalists don't use the words* I *or* me *much.*

---

[7]It was, I believe, the Chinese army that invented hierarchy in ancient times. The most layers they ever had numbered ten. Burger King had passed that, and almost reached the organizational complexity and depth of the average city mayor's office in the U.S.

still in the sky; and some kid working the drive-through window for minimum wage on the midnight shift in downtown Detroit while the big guns were home in bed. Al, baby, you're not Michael Jackson. This is a team game.

If that moan is about style, my second and bigger beef is about substance. Dunlap's ingoing (and outgoing) position is that shareholder value is all-important. For him, nothing else matters and there is no room for misunderstanding. There is, of course, only one class of shareholder, the financial investor who buys equity in a company. Anything and everything Dunlap does is justified if it increases the return to that interested party (in either distributed dividends or capital appreciation), preferably in the short term. No other investors are recognized. All the bread must be fed to the frenzied, feeding, stockholder ducks.

I'm not going to argue that, in the case of a single patient needing a triple amputation to survive, you should start getting fancy about multiple goals. But I'm going to argue like hell that we should not make Dunlap an icon and advocate mass amputation and single stakeholder worship as a proactive way of keeping the vast majority of businesses effective and efficient and away from life-threatening illness.

The time has long gone when you could look at the complex cast and relationships that make up a modern business and plan a route to sustainable prosperity by rolling a six on the dice of one party with the rest having to make do with a one.

Sure, stockholders invest in a company, but so do many others:

◆ Take people who join a company in their twenties and stay until they're past forty. Sure, they're paid a salary (just like a dividend) but don't you think they have invested in the balance sheet as well? Doesn't it count for something that the most productive years of a life have contributed to the corporate cause? Contrast Dunlap's approach to these second-class citizens with Southwest Airline's Herb Kellerher's refusal to lay off workers when fuel prices went through the roof during the Gulf War, even though much of his competition was laying off. The reason was simple: He never even contemplated it. Ooops! Bang goes a couple of short-term cents on the earnings per share, but last time I looked Southwest Airlines was a picture of health.

♦ Let's see how Dunlap's magic dust might work in a franchised system such as Burger King. Here we have the oddity that the franchisees have more money in total invested in the system than the conventional stockholders.[8] It doesn't sound like a good idea (to me) to rob the 'zees to make sure the stockholders get every available penny, because franchised systems only grow on the backs of wealthy and happy franchisees. Yeah, yeah, I know they would never admit to that state even if they were in it, but trust me on this one. For once I know what I'm talking about.

♦ Talking of investors, has anybody calculated just how much the suppliers and vendors of (say) McDonald's or General Motors have invested in the system and need to keep investing to keep the system competitive? So, it's okay if we squeeze them dry to jack up the earnings, is it? Ray Kroc felt the way to sustainable healthy growth in McDonald's was via pretty much the opposite way of dealing with suppliers, and he worked on a win–win handshake deal with most of them. Last time I looked the Golden Arches were alive and kicking, and have managed to deliver to their stockholders over the years.

♦ Let's go pinky-liberal. Isn't the community (or planet, or whatever) an investor as well? In Florida, the community (or planet, or whatever) combined to give the sugar growers perfect conditions to make their conventional shareholders very wealthy. However, by optimizing conventional stockholder returns, the community or planet investor got a lousy deal in return, in the form of poisoned Everglades, and the conventional stockholders are now squealing like stuck pigs because they have been asked to pay to clean it up. (Hee, hee!) So I guess we'd all better shut up. We don't want growers suboptimizing returns, do we?

♦ Finally, what about the consumer as another kind of investor? Maybe you only invest by buying a car or an airline ticket, so I guess it's okay if the auto makers and airlines cut

---

[8]Franchisees tend to remind you of this fact. About every twenty minutes or so.

back a bit on safety spending to keep Pat Stockholder happy. On the other hand, maybe you've invested in four packs of cigarettes a day for all your adult life, and just maybe the tobacco companies have now killed more of you than Hitler and Stalin combined, but you're still not really a *proper* investor, are you? So it's okay if Big Tobacco keeps putting the telescope to its blind eye to protect stockholders' value. Well, isn't it?

**Universal Law #19**

*Business is a complex interaction between the investments of conventional stockholders, employees, communities, vendors, agents, distributors, licensors, retailers, and end users. All add value; and healthy, sustainable wealth creation can only come from the enlightened balancing of a fair return to all.*

I bow to no one in my support of a free market and wealth creation. The Invisible Hand economic theory works for me. I am a champion of the need for constant reinvention and the need to be effective and efficient. It was tough, I know, on the dinosaurs and the dodo, but Darwinism rules, in nature and in business. I am an advocate of constant change—daily, hourly if necessary—to prevent corporate illness by a constant, vigorous process of evolution rather than reacting to it by massive revolution. All of the above are part of modern business life, but today's corporation is not about one-dimensional stockholding and its rewards. The organization is a complex interaction between the investments of stockholders, employees, communities, vendors, agents, distributors, licensors, retailers, and end users. All add value; healthy, sustainable wealth creation will only come from the enlightened balancing of a fair return to all.

For some, the key to enlightened capitalism seems to lie in a fortune cookie kind of approach: If you write down (in sound bites) where you are going, what you stand for, and how you want the business done (etc.) and post that on appropriate walls, then it will become a self-fulfilling prophecy. I refer, of course, to corporate vision, mission and value statements. They are, almost without exception, a total crock. When they eventually build the business Hall of Fame, my vote for the first member will go to Lou Gerstner, the savior of IBM. Not for what he has achieved there (and elsewhere), but for his immortal remark when asked about his vision for IBM when he took over. The company, if you remember, was in a rotten mess, and his reply that the last thing IBM needed was a vision went down badly with a lot of folks. For me, it was the stuff heroes are made of; a vision is the last thing *most* companies need.

Enlightened mission, vision, and value statements do not make for enlightened capitalism. In fact they are frequently counterproductive, pompous, written for the wrong audiences, and unworkable.

**Universal Law #20**

*Enlightened mission, vision, and value statements do not make for enlightened capitalism. In fact they are often counterproductive. They're the* last *thing most companies need.*

True story: Late in 1988 I arrived at Burger King's world headquarters in Florida to take over as CEO after my U.K. company (GrandMet) took Burger King over via a (hotly) contested acquisition. My appointment was not announced publicly until the day of my arrival from England and, after a short introductory chat with the management team, I went to my office. Understandably, there was not a file or piece of paper left behind in it, and it was a rather eerie feeling walking around a huge office that was devoid of human touches. Hanging on the wall was the Pillsbury mission statement (Burger King was owned by Pillsbury), and in my desperation to digest anything I read it avidly. I passed about six split infinitives ("to boldly go...") and a load of politically correct humbug and suddenly started laughing. It was a real tension breaker for me. The joke was that if they'd lived by half of what was written down, I would not have been there.

Now let me confuse everybody by stating that the cause of enlightened capitalism can be helped in general by something really weird: dreams! Specifically, by dreams that the lawyers won't let you put down in writing, even if you wanted to. Here's another true story to help explain: A couple of years after I arrived at Burger King, a woman came from out

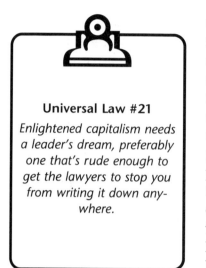

of town to our headquarters for a job interview. This process, which included a meeting with me, came and went and she got the job. It wasn't till later that I found out she had arrived in a taxi at our gate and discovered she had no money, at which point our security guard paid the fare out of his own pocket and made sure she had enough for the (eventual) return journey so she didn't have to worry about that during the interviews. When I (fortuitously) heard of this, I stared into space for a long time, because the security guard had captured what I was trying to achieve with Burger King. The restaurants, the food and the marketing, all that complex stuff that's behind providing a burger and fries at a food counter was coming along fine, but something was missing. We had 250,000 people working in the system worldwide, and if we could just get them to think and care like that security guard we would be so different. I shaped my personal dream: a quarter of a million people in Burger King, *and every one of them gives a shit.*

No, the lawyers wouldn't let me print it, but it was enormously helpful to me to define what I wanted from everybody in the system—accounting, purchasing, marketing, operations, whatever. I made sure all the people I met with knew my dream (or a publishable version of it!).[9]

---

[9]Sadly, the lawyers were probably quite right. When we launched the Burger King ad campaign, "Sometimes you gotta break the rules," it was a similar dream, this time invented by my wife and originally pointed at American retail in general after she couldn't cash a check in a supermarket because our American driving licenses hadn't come through. We stole the line from her, and thought it would express one of our competitive edges, breaking the fast food rules by broiling instead of frying and by making the sandwiches individually instead of en masse. What we got was lots of grief from assorted religious groups and PTAs charging us with leading America astray by advocating mass anarchy on the TV. It is one of my great regrets that I didn't go to my corporate death via an insistence that we air "Burger King: We *all* give a shit" at halftime during the Super Bowl.

Hegel, the gloomy German philosopher, theorized that liberal views come and go on a thirty-year swing. It may well be that the time is right for a more balanced (enlightened) role for capitalism. It is more likely, however, that progress will be spurred by the force that has driven all forward momentum in capitalism, that of vested self-interest. Johnson & Johnson, the world's largest health care company, functions with deliberately redundant operations and amazingly independent management, all held together by its own stringent system of ethics that places profits and stockholders dead last. Its earnings are among the industry's best. Southwest Airlines seems to score highest on the most variables in the balanced, enlightened model, and the company is a model of efficiency, safety, and earnings growth. And, of course, Dunlap got canned,[10] so there is hope.

The key is the equal pursuit of the three goals—doing more, in a better way, with less—in a mixture of technical skill and spiritual enterprise. We should not celebrate doing less, in a worse way, with less, as any kind of victory, although we should recognize that might be the only way to survive in specific circumstances. We should not make the managers who do this into role models or use business turnarounds achieved by Dunlap's methods for business school case studies. When you look into your tool box and see you only have a hammer, every problem or opportunity tends to look like a nail. Enlightened capitalists have lots of tools.

---

[10]Many people ask me how long I laughed when I heard this news and frankly, it's difficult to be accurate. My wife timed the first phase at two hours and thirty-two minutes, but then I realized that all the investors who had followed Wall Street's Mr. Bean would take a bath with him on Sunbeam stock. That added another forty minutes, for a total of three hours and twelve minutes.

# 4

## On Limited Terms
## for Business Leaders

I'm generally an easygoing guy who can see the funny side of most things, but there are some sights in the modern world that depress the hell out of me. Driving through the First World War battlefields in northern France and seeing the war graves is a profoundly moving experience for me, and I only have to see the entrance to a EuroDisney to be upset for weeks. The saddest sight of all, however, in my book, is to see Mohammed Ali deteriorating in his sunset years.

I know many people accept the diagnosis that he is simply one of those unfortunate people who have drawn the short straw of Parkinson's disease and that boxing had nothing to do with his physical and mental deterioration. I cannot accept that boxing played no part in it, and I shall always wonder whether I directly contributed to his downfall during our three world championship fights during the early seventies. As I remember it, the tabloid press (rather primitively) christened the third (deciding) fight we staged in Malaysia "the Thumper in Kuala Lumpur," and it is amazing how different people recall different things about that famous night. I, of course, remember little, as I measured my length on the canvas after four seconds.

As the world knows I quit boxing there and then and launched my career as a Captain of Industry. It saddens me to see Mohammed today, with his dancing feet reduced to a shuffle and his acerbic articulation now an agonizing slur. Did the one punch I managed to land on his forearm (during the pre-fight national anthems) play some part in that sorrowful metamorphosis? Perhaps. But perhaps the more relevant question is: Did he stay on too long in boxing?

We see it over and over again in every walk of life—people staying on in a position or set of circumstances well beyond their welcome or capabilities (and probably their own enjoyment and satisfaction). Unnecessary shadows are cast on hard-earned successes and reputations because these folks simply will not quit while they are ahead. In my adopted home of south Florida, the mid-nineties gave us the classic example of Don Shula, the Miami Dolphin's football coach, an example that enables us to ask all the easy questions but doesn't provide any (quite so) easy answers. Here we have a guy gloriously heralded in the U.S. media as the winningest coach in NFL history. (Author's note: I may have this wrong. It might be the coachingest winninger in the sport's history, but no matter. Both bear the same relationship to correct English). Shula was the guy who gave football its only perfect season. He was the coach's coach, with the respect of everybody else in the game and a jillion others outside of it. But those last unnecessary couple of years now taint the memory, years of over-promise and under-delivery, barely managed locker-room divisions, overpaid veteran players out of control (and past their own sell-by dates) and sulking to the press, with everybody blaming everybody else.

Shula left with his contract unfinished. The spin doctors worked overtime but the signals were clear: It was more "push" than "jump." The great man was replaced by a younger coach wearing a track suit,[1] who suddenly seemed to be doing the oh-so-obvious right things.

Shula did not become a failure overnight. Out of respect, everybody (rightly) accentuated the positive, cherry-picking the career highlights. When the history of the game is written in a

---

[1]And a wondrously appalling hairstyle.

hundred years, Shula's paragraph will read well. But he must know, as does everybody else, that he did not depart from the game leaving anything on the table.

So far I have used a couple of sporting examples to define the issue, but it manifests itself in most aspects of life. One exception exists, however, a result of the vision of a few who recognized this issue, saw it coming, and deduced that if they didn't design a structure that would guarantee its defeat, it could have profound negative implications for a nation.

I refer, of course, to the visionary gentlemen who shaped the postwar governance of the United States of America, and their insistence on *limited terms* in the highest political office in the land. I write today in the shadow of Clinton's reign of terror, but safe in the knowledge that he must eventually join me on the lecture tour. I guess in the distant future we will look back on him with some sort of benevolent fondness.[2]

Term limits can be critical in determining success. During the 1980s, the U.S. and the U.K. were led by two people with very similar ideologies: Ronald Reagan and Margaret Thatcher. Few would argue that the latter's intellectual capacity qualified her to leave a more successful scorch mark on the fabric of history than the error-prone B-movie star. But he did his allotted time and rode off into the sunset, and many were sad to see him go. Here we have a guy who, armed only with a Norman Rockwell-meets-Bugs Bunny communication style and an Adam Smith-meets-Madge-in-a-trailer-park economic doctrine, has left us with a memory of what many term a golden period.

What of Thatcher? Here's a thought: If she too had been limited to her first eight years, she would have gone down in history as one of Britain's finest prime ministers and would have my vote for the top spot. She gave a quite astonishing performance of true leadership, but neither the system nor her own nature provided a mandatory or obvious successor, so she stayed on. And on and on and on. Eventually she became isolated in her own party, out of touch with the nation, and a sad parody of herself. She began giving off what many of us believe were

[2]This happens, trust me. Apparently Nixon now slots in between Mother Theresa and Saint Bob Geldof in historic perspective.

the first symptoms of mad cow disease. If Reagan had stayed? Does anyone doubt that the thing would have ended unhappily and the U.S. would have had to use a crowbar to get him out?

It is not hard to draw parallels in business. In fact the condition is so prevalent it now has its own name: the Kenneth Olsen syndrome. He was the founder and longtime CEO of Digital Equipment until he was forced out of DEC in 1992, and it's fair to say he had been one of the networked-systems industry's visionaries. But it's also fair to say he did not adjust well to a rapidly changing business environment and lost it completely. Around the time of his leaving he dropped a sound bite to *Fortune* magazine that tells it all: "You can be sure our plan was perfect; it's just that the assumptions were wrong." Ouch.[3] There are many more examples of this disease (Robert Allen of AT&T?), but we steadfastly refuse to learn the lessons. Leaders are appointed on open-ended contracts and usually only leave because they are so successful they are headhunted elsewhere, or they have failed (or are failing). The former situation is a mess because it is seen as interrupting (and therefore threatening) success, and the latter is a mess because it's a mess. When you hear of a three-year contract of employment being signed, it is has nothing to do with the expected term of work; it represents a formula to define compensation (one way or another) should the leader be pushed or pulled.

**Universal Law #22**

*The Sigmoid curve will apply, so either get out of a situation or profoundly reinvent it, just before the curve peaks.*

Charles Handy (I confess I am a disciple) reminds us of the need to reinvent, or move on from, anything—job, relationship, state of mind, stage of life—before the sigmoid curve peaks and turns downward.[4] This is a flat-on-its-side, S-shaped curve that governs most things in life. There is a little wiggle at the start, then a significant rise to a

---

[3]DEC continued to struggle until recently, when they had the wisdom to employ me to give a management seminar. That finished them completely—soon after they were swallowed up by Compaq.

[4]Charles Handy, *The Empty Raincoat* (Hutchinson, 1994).

(rounded) peak, followed by a downward tail-off.[5] The key is to either profoundly reinvent the situation or get out of it just before the absolute peak occurs. Where business is concerned, both options usually necessitate a change of leader.

But what of the counterargument, that continuity and stability are undervalued in today's madhouse of change? That change for change's sake is part of today's problem, not the solution? That short-term hired guns cannot bring the causal commitment and deep understanding that long-term associates bring? How 'bout Roberto Goizuetta's long (and glorious) reign at Coca-Cola? I don't think the argument succeeds. Some exceptions prove the rule, but for every Goizuetta[6] there is a gaggle of Allens and Olsens.

A number of symptoms indicate the presence of the disease of staying beyond your corporate shelf life. They're not difficult to spot and they (mostly) manifest themselves as variations on a theme of complacency. In my case they were visible with a simple look in the mirror if I stayed anyplace for longer than four or five years.

The first telltale sign is a growing tendency for *self-parody*. I think it was Errol Flynn (if it wasn't, it should have been) who said: "The trouble with Humphrey Bogart is that, after eleven o'clock at night, he thinks he's Humphrey Bogart." When Johnny Mathis started singing years ago, his voice had an occasional distinct inflection, which he used very sparingly.[7] It obviously didn't annoy about a jillion women because today everything he does is built on it. What happened to these two is what happens to every leader: People respond to the things you do, positively

---

[5]It's interesting to test this with your own relationship or career experiences. It works particularly well when I relate it to eating nouvelle cuisine (except that the peak comes early—very early).

[6]Roberto Goizuetta died in 1997. I met him a few times during my tenure with Burger King. He just seemed to get better with the years, like a quality claret. I don't think he blew the S curve theory up, because I believe he was still ascending, but his curve was probably the widest plotted since records began. He was, therefore, an exception that proves the rule.

[7]I remember it because it really annoyed me. Still does.

and negatively, and gradually you provide them with more of what they want. It may be unconscious, but it happens.

In business a behavioral mannerism, a style factor, or a particular way of going about your work that was once intuitive becomes a formula. A mixture of pull and push is at play; the leader provides it, the people react positively and expect more of the same. So more is provided even if the circumstances are not quite as appropriate, and the cycle is repeated until the distortion factor is material. The superficial substitutes for the substantial, and dogma substitutes for analysis.

**Universal Law #23**

*Never accept the following logic: We're doing it this way because that's how we've always done it, or We're not doing it 'cos we've never done it. Have your staff tattoo this (high) on their inner thighs.*

The business downside of this symptom is, of course, the temptation to repeat successful formulas because they worked once. When people joined my team I asked them to tattoo the following universal law high on their inner thighs: There are two reasons we will never accept for anything: We won't do it because we've never done it, and We'll do it because we've (always) done it this way. They are both sure signs the S curve is heading south.

The second symptom is the search for *comfort zones*. I was lucky to have two mentors during a lot of my time in business, and remember one of them advising me: Never employ anyone who is not capable of hitting you. Notwithstanding the double negative, it's about the soundest single piece of advice I've heard, and a similar rule might be: Never take the easiest option available. That's the kind of thinking that moved Michelangelo to paint the Sistine Chapel *ceiling* instead of the floor or walls as you or I would have done.[8]

**Universal Law #24**

*Learn to hate comfort. Only hire people who are capable of hitting you; set outrageous goals for yourself; ban yourself from taking the easiest option for anything. Remember, Michelangelo chose to paint the Sistine Chapel ceiling.*

---

[8]In my particular case I would also have used a roller.

However strong leader figures are, they have a tendency over time to surround themselves with folks who aren't capable of hitting them and to choose high-percentage business options. You form attachments to people and projects for the wrong reasons, in the same way you discard people and options for the wrong reasons. In golfing parlance, you lay up on the par fives. Welcome to the comfort zone.

What also happens in this zone is that (previously) stretched or even outrageous goal setting retracts to levels at which the goals are achievable with comfort or are very loosely defined (e.g., "Start ad campaign by July"). The familiarity and accrued competence mean you can set targets you know will get accomplished, both for yourself and for your team, pretty much by just showing up for work. If this symptom spreads, it's as near as business gets to having terminal cancer.

Next, you can easily spot the *reinvention or maintenance* symptom. After a ten-year run on Broadway, with box office receipts showing no sign of dropping off, Sir Cameron Macintosh, the producer of *Cats*, stunned the world of show business (and a few peripheral ones) by firing more than a third of the cast. He said he'd spotted signs of long-run-itis, a disease that should be written about and covered in every business school in the West.

How many of us in business, whether in a mighty corporation or a small project team, would have the moxie to do that? We'd be even less likely to do it if we'd been around at the start, put the people in place personally, and shared the success on the way. The temptation is to leave a situation alone, then fix it when a leak appears, and keep fixing it and fixing it. That may involve tough decisions measured by the leader's ruler, but they may not be enough to keep winning in the marketplace. A new leader, of course, has few fears about reinvention. In fact, quite the opposite: A new leader fears maintaining the predecessor's status quo.

Rather embarrassingly, some rock stars can teach business a thing or two about high-risk (but essential) reinvention. Many people feel that Paul Simon peaked when he wrote and performed *Bridge Over Troubled Waters* to celebrate an early midlife crisis of mine, but he followed up his partnership with

Garfunkel by continuing a career of constant reinvention. Solo performing, blending with different ethnic influences, and Broadway musicals all played a part in keeping him on the right side of the S curve peak.

Next symptom? A leader with an evergreen contract and a hang-on philosophy does not pay adequate attention to *succession planning*, and neither do those who are also paid to do so. Another piece of wisdom that has had a manifest influence on my business life came from my second mentor (remember, there were two!): On the first day of any new appointment, a new leader should take time out from the noise and clutter to identify a successor. Then fire the bastard. We will not, for obvious reasons, include this as a universal law, although there is reason to believe it is popular in its own right.

This was Thatcher's heinous crime in my book, for I believe it to be a fundamental of any leader's challenge to plan for his or her own succession. That's how you supply continuity in management. If you're on an evergreen deal, it's very difficult to do. You end up developing an overt contingency succession plan that nobody is really committed to because they don't want it to happen. The Board Nominating Committee or some external executive structure might do some covert planning and talk about a few names, but that's usually only done when the situation's already in free fall.

**Universal Law #25**

*Leadership succession planning must start on appointment. Succession should involve neither surprise nor panic.*

Contrast that with the situation in which a leader is taken on openly and honestly for a fixed term, and on a predetermined future date he or she will leave the business, leaving history to mark the scorecard. Succession planning becomes open, honest, real, and essential—a hundred times more healthy than the shadowboxing and shenanigans normally associated with this activity. Succession should not involve about panic or surprise. One of the greatest achievements of Goizuetta was that the stock market responded to his untimely death without a blip, so efficient had he (and the board) been in grooming Doug Ivester to succeed him. We may yet see the triumphs of Bill Gates and Michael Eisner dimmed by their failings in this area.

The last symptoms of a leader who has stayed too long in the ring are *too few signs of crisis* and *too many signs of success.* A long run in a job can result in a (business) captain and crew who steer around most surface icebergs, almost by second nature—and that can be a bad thing. A quite regular crisis can be just what the business needs to keep its competitive edge honed, sorting out who will contribute under fire and who will wilt, forcing new solutions, getting the adrenalin going again, stretching personal performance, and so on. The converse is that a long leadership run can bring dangerous subliminal messages that all is well and successful. The boardroom gets a new marble table that could double as a heliport, corporate lifestyles get richer (and softer), and the message creeps out: We're rich, we're successful. Let's have lunch.

I expect to be howled down again for these proposals by people who believe Ali left me a few sandwiches short of a picnic. Is it right in one essay to challenge the foundations of the way business employs its leaders?

I wish to be remembered for two things. In my prime (everything is relative) I scored three goals at soccer, playing in England against the Internal Revenue Service's elite London team. On a glorious fall afternoon, sometime in the mid 1970s, I struck a savage counterblow for the

**Universal Law # 26**

*If you haven't had a crisis for a while, invent one.*

**Universal Law #27**

*Ban all signs of success from (day-to-day) view.*

world's overtaxed. I also want to be remembered for proposing fixed terms for executives—two terms and you're out.

Now, the more perceptive among you will have deduced that I am not actually advocating limited terms as ends in themselves, but as means to an end. I do deem it essential that a leader quit before the S curve peaks and falls, because all or many of the symptoms I describe rapidly become self-evident when that happens. I accept that in some exceptional cases it can take many years (decades even) for some leaders to reach that position. But in the vast majority of cases, long-run-itis sets in after a maximum of eight to ten years. Limited terms are simply mechanisms to force recognition and action that will benefit most businesses in most cases. The framers of the U.S. Constitution decided this was the best way to manage the risk for the nation as far as its leadership was concerned, and they were right.

Setting term limits for leaders demands a totally different way of compensating them, but that's a detail. Term limits will finally kill off the idea of womb-to-tomb employment with one organization, but that's dying anyway. Term limits will create change and turbulence where none are viewed as necessary, in a world where we already experience change overload. It will be pointed out that some leaders will undoubtedly leave office before their best work is finished. Others will attack the idea as a hired-gun culture and another nail in the coffin of the Golden Age of business.

What drivel. The benefits will be huge. A two-term period with a fixed exit date at the end will be hugely advantageous in keeping Western business alive, alert, and competitive.

I used DEC's Kenneth Olsen an example and, okay, I picked an easy one. So let me finish with one that many will see as one degree short of heresy—a proposal that Bill Gates has passed his sell-by date with Microsoft. After all, Gates is Microsoft and has led it from its genesis to a market value bigger than General Motors.[9] Surely the company would die on the vine without him?

---

[9]And possibly a higher personal net worth than most gods.

I don't think so. Sure, Gates saw the future in distributed personal computer operating systems and beat IBM to it. But he nearly missed the boat when cheap modems suddenly made the Web a consumer product and he looks uncomfortable about facing the advent of the true network PC. Time for a change on the bridge of the good ship Microsoft? As with many of the truly healthy options open to business today, it requires thinking the unthinkable.

I would never associate with a business again without a fixed exit arrangement, but that's redundant. I have plans elsewhere. If George Foreman can do it, so can I, and I'm planning a boxing comeback. My agent and (third) mentor, Don King, is finalizing arrangements for me to take a shot at one of the rather complex new titles in the sport: the World, Universe, and Interplanetary Boxing Confederation and Liaison Association Committee's Relatively Super Gross Heavyweight (WUIB-CLACRSGH) title, in Las Vegas next year. Projected opponent: Dolly Parton.

# On Being Big
# but Acting SMALL

I have never yet seen (or heard of) a plane reversing into a mountain, which is why I believe the first class compartment should be at the back. If you are going to pay all that money, shouldn't you get the safest as well as the best seats?

This is one of the many, many things airlines get wrong.[1] For the consumer, commercial flight represents one of the biggest gaps between what could be and what is in business today, led by the arrogance of the major airlines and their take-it-or-leave-it approach to the market. They are big companies thinking like big companies, the icons of a supply-side mentality.

It doesn't have to be this way, of course, and there are a few exceptions appearing on the radar screen that might lead the whole industry into a different way of thinking. Here are two true stories that indicate a difference in approach that might have profound implications for the future of the industry.

---

[1]Another one: In the history of domestic flight in the U.S., it is estimated that the chances of two people on the same plane actually paying the same price for their tickets are the same as the DNA samples left by O. J. Simpson being explainable.

First, a buddy of mine was flying out from England to visit us in Miami, a nine-hour haul on one of the big international carriers. Midway across the Atlantic, some technical trouble developed that necessitated that they turn back. Now here's the first master stroke: They didn't tell anybody. Nine hours after takeoff, as they approached the runway to land, everybody looked out of the window expecting to see Miami Beach and millions of cubic feet of cleavage. Instead they saw the River Thames and Windsor Castle.[2] You can imagine the consternation and the questions to be answered: What about the cruise I was going to catch? My connecting flight? What about my granny who was meeting me at the airport?...And so on. Here's where the airline pulled the second master stroke of the day: They had one small desk and only two people handling all this as people disembarked. It took more than an hour to get off the plane.

That strikes me as how it shouldn't be done: a big company giving off all the signals that it should be considered a privilege to fly with them.

Contrast this with a trip going the other way, this time by a relative of ours returning to the U.K. after staying with us. When we got to Miami airport we were greeted by the depressing news that the flight had been delayed four hours—just what you need with a long, overnight flight ahead. Everybody was tense and wandering about moaning and groaning until a bunch of folks in airline uniforms started handing out sheets of paper to everybody. It was a copy of a fax that had just arrived from England. It was a personal note *signed by the chairman of the airline* explaining what had gone wrong, what they were doing to fix it, and what would happen next and listing some things they were doing to make life as comfortable as possible in the interim. The fax was timed in the early hours of the morning (U.K. time) and the effect on my relative was astonishing: You would think she'd just been handed a winning lottery ticket.

Now, crowd in a bit here because I'm only going to whisper the next bit. You know what I think? I think they didn't get the chairman out of bed at all. I may be totally wrong (in which

---

[2]Not well known for cleavage. At least, not officially.

case the example is even better) but I think the airline had devised a process in advance so that whenever they had a problem anywhere in the world a personal fax from the chairman winged its way to the trouble spot. Brilliant.

What you have here is a big company thinking like a small company, and it will come as no surprise to many of you that the airline in the second story was Virgin, whose chairman is Richard Branson. (The first one will remain unnamed, although I'll give you some clues: It is a huge airline, and *British* is part of its two-word title.) Virgin is a big company all right, with 9500 employees, 120 businesses, and revenues in excess of $2.5 billion. But somehow you feel you're never far away from the "proprietor" and if there's a problem the "shopkeeper" will appear to solve it. I'm no great fan of Branson as a person (it's that silly beard and that annoying, ever-present grin), but I have a deep respect for his intuitive approach to business. He has a very approachable personal style: He has no handlers, retinue, or bodyguard to shield him from contact. He stays in the same hotel as his flight crew, talks to everyone, and tries to remember everybody's first names. Branson has made it an imperative of the business to "act small," which requires policies and procedures to make it happen such as splitting the 3000-member cabin crew into 20 groups of 150 each that always fly together. As Branson said in an interview in *Esquire* magazine in 1996, "As we get bigger, we try to get smaller."

Not every company is led by a Richard Branson, but I'm not sure such leadership from the top is a must-have to achieve many of the same effects. What I am sure about is that the ability to think small (or local) is key to the future marketing of big brands, and I think we can take one of our universal laws from Branson's midnight fax inspiration: Involve the head of the business in frontline service issues, even if he or she doesn't know about it!

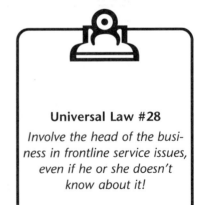

**Universal Law #28**

*Involve the head of the business in frontline service issues, even if he or she doesn't know about it!*

One huge problem at Burger King was that there seemed to be little room for maneuvering from the brand specification. God knows we had enough problems around the early 1990s trying to get restaurant operators just to deliver the brand products properly to the customer. The notion of adding their own local micro-market touch was incomprehensible to many operators. I remember visiting Chicago with the local district manager, and insisting that we visit a restaurant run by a rogue franchisee. As we entered the place sometime around breakfast he all but crumpled in front of me as we were greeted by a long line at the register, all shouting, grinning, and being generally disorderly. This, of course, was not how a Burger King should have been at that time in its history.[3] The reason for the disturbance quickly became clear. On the wall behind the register the operator had hung a small toy basketball hoop, the kind you pitch a light sponge "basketball" through. Everyone who came in got one try to sink a free throw and if you made the shot, your coffee was free. The customers were loving it.

The district manager sprang a leak. I'm convinced I saw gear box oil coming out of his nose as he set off toward the crowd, assured in his own mind (I assume) that the only hope he had of rescuing his doomed career was to fire everybody in the place and possibly shoot a few as well. I grabbed his coat sleeve and calmed him down. When he had regained control, I asked him what he saw when he looked at this spectacle, and gradually the message dawned on him: What we had was a crowd of customers (not common in Burger King then). We also had a crowd having fun, we had a place that was alive, and we clearly had incremental business. The cost of this "promotion" (a few free

**Universal Law #29**

*The bigger your brand, the more your tactical marketing and service must reflect the local (micro) market.*

---

[3] I think the idea was that it should have been quiet. And empty.

cups of coffee) was pennies,[4] but I had a hell of a job convincing my manager that this was a good thing. To me it was a splendid example of a local executive responsible for delivering a mega-brand to the market, adding some micro-market distinction, and making the whole package that little bit more attractive. We had a big company thinking small, and that will be an imperative if you are to compete effectively in the future. The bigger you are, the more you will need local flexibility to add further value to your products and services.

Small touches can have tremendous impact, and the key variable is service: developing the relationship you have locally with the customer. Often in big companies there is little you can do to vary the product specification or price. But you have a huge opportunity to adapt to the local consumer through tactical marketing and service.

This is a critical challenge for big companies and their megabrands. As consumers show less tolerance for mass marketing and more insistence that their own values and needs be respected, the ability of the giants to be flexible will be crucial to their continuing competitiveness. By the year 2000, 85 percent of the labor force will be working for firms employing fewer than 200 people, providing a plethora of goods and services on an intimate, flexible local market level. Attracting and retaining the best talent will be a key issue, and big companies that can only think "big" are in for a tougher time in the future. Here's a Peter Drucker prediction that might shake those of you who can't see past the blue chips: They will no longer be able to attract the best and brightest for their management ranks. In an interview in *Fortune* magazine (March 1997) Drucker stated, "Most of my former students are bored working for large com-

[4]The profit margin on Burger King coffee used to be the second highest in the whole food and beverage industry, beaten only by Mexican refried beans. Operators would often brew a pot of coffee and it would remain on the hot plate for weeks, with customers getting quite emotional and having memorial services when it was finally replaced. Author's update: The advent of the $5 bottle of water may have changed the rankings here. I paid that in a restaurant recently and was then deflected from concentrating on my meal by the thought of what my grandparents would have made of it all. Talking of bottled water, when did it become mandatory to carry a supply of water when shopping in the mall on the weekend? Have I missed something? Has Macy's become the risk equivalent of crossing the Gobi Desert?

panies, and they switch to medium-size and small companies after a few years. The only reason they take jobs at large companies is they're the only ones recruiting on campus."

For years now the air has been full of the whinging and whining of the American automobile manufacturers, complaining that they don't get a level playing field when they (try to) trade in Japan. Rubbish. The key to the door to the Japanese market is right inside this "act big, act small" concept. The positions are so crystallized, however, it looks like I may have to intervene and I suppose I will only be able to do that from the highest level.

So this is a good time for me to give America a foretaste of what is to come when I'm president. Colin Powell has given me the nod to be his running mate in the year 2004, the plan being that I succeed him in 2012 after a suitable constitutional amendment allowing Brits into the White House. The interim years will also give Colin plenty of time to learn to pronounce his first name correctly.

When I'm in power—hear it *now*, America—two things will happen fast: First, a mandatory, no appeal, death penalty will be introduced for restaurant staff who sing "Happy Birthday" to diners. Second, I will fix, for once and all time, the automobile trading relationship between the U.S. and Japan.

I've had many sleepless nights over the last few years, sweating, tossing, and turning while the sound of manic Nippon laughter rang round my brain. Their joy, of course, is a result of their own "compromise" in the face of terrifying threats from, by now, a number of American presidents to raise tariffs on the import of luxury cars into the U.S. unless the Japanese opened their own home markets further to Detroit's finest. In the good ol' days of George Bush, this was accompanied by the negotiating tactic of barfing in the Japanese prime minister's lap over dinner. This was followed, I understand, by Bill Clinton misunderstanding the ancient tea ceremony and suggesting something entirely different to his hostess. In any case, the various Japanese delegations nodded in the way only they can nod and agreed to change their protective trading practices. Solemnly.

Now, read the next bit carefully: *I don't think any of them have given up anything of any significance.* Certainly any gains made by U.S. auto makers were too small to show up on radar, hence the manic Japanese laughter.

We will not pause long in reflection here, for there is actually a much bigger problem: The Japanese needn't worry anyway; they don't have any real need to protect their market so fiercely. If they shifted every tangible and intangible barrier in the way, I don't believe America would actually penetrate their market much more because the real issues remain on this side of the Pacific. You don't shift years and years of inadequate management attitude, and its consequences, overnight.

Talking of inadequate management, I read a biography of Iacocca[5] on a long plane journey recently and at long last found someone who shares my views and celebrated with a second bag of American Airlines' proprietary peanuts (What happened to airline food? Was it something we said?). For those of you taking notes here, let me summarize my views[6]: Iacocca, the mythical American corporate icon, was for long periods while he was at the helm of Chrysler actually a shallow, self-serving, myopic part of America's *problems*, not its solutions. If America needs a role model hero for the rescue of Chrysler in the early eighties, then it should go look in the mirror. The taxpayer bailed Chrysler out. End of topic.

More to the point of the current debate, when Chrysler was liquid and up and running again, Uncle Lee failed to learn the lesson and keep pace with our friends under the Rising Sun. But he always had a helluva nice jet.

Iacocca and Chrysler are not alone. They have been in good company with the other Big Two and other auto makers in Europe. They are all true global brands, but they still make the mistake of both thinking *and* acting globally, whereas the key is to think globally but act as a local outfit. This is a good rule for anywhere, but don't leave home without it if you want to compete in Japan.

[5]Doron P. Levin, *Behind the Wheel at Chrysler* (Harcourt Brace, 1996).

[6]On automobiles, not peanuts. My view on peanuts on planes is simple: They should be banned because they are a safety hazard. Or at least they are when I've eaten 'em.

Of course megabranding is about consistency of trademark, values, and core specifications, but your tactical marketing and service support programs must reflect local conditions. Green Giant canned corn is marketed in France as a cold salad item; twenty-two miles away in England it is marketed as a hot vegetable. Same product, same package, but entirely different consumer markets, as you'd expect from two nations that have technically been at war for 700 years.[7]

Back to Japan and cars: The local market has two fundamental distinctions for automobile marketing. First, in common with the Brits (Okay! Okay!), the Japanese drive on the left side of the road, which drops an ever-so-gentle hint that the steering wheel should be on the right side of the car. That does not mean the correct side of the car, it means the one that isn't on the left. In turn, that should not mean that right-hand drive is an expensive additional option; it should be the rule, not the exception. The second distinction is that selling cars in Japan is a different process in a different infrastructure from the U.S. They have few of the expensive, high-acreage (and high-inventory) dealerships that poison the landscape of suburban America. Instead, car sales are largely made by thousands of salespeople who visit the homes and offices of their customers and who have built relationships over years and years of repeat business. It is a different way of doing business and one that is alien to the West, but when that's what happens in Rome, you gotta do what the Romans do. (I was going to say "When in Tokyo do as the Tokyans do," but it doesn't

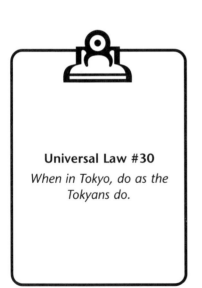

**Universal Law #30**

*When in Tokyo, do as the Tokyans do.*

---

[7]This is true. I have traced a war between England and France back then, and we never declared peace. Due to the restrictive policies of NATO, however, we limit our modern hostilities to sending the odd busload of soccer fans across to each other, which is usually good for flattening a couple of provincial towns. In fairness, though, we Brits have now built a tunnel under the Channel so that the French can surrender a lot more effectively and efficiently.

sound right. On the other hand, these are my universal laws, not yours....)

The good news is that, brand for brand and, encouragingly, quality for quality, there's not much difference between U.S. and Japanese cars now. In the U.S., however, the Japanese take their global brands and work within the mechanics and processes of the American local market and they do it as well as we do. In fact, let's be honest here: Frequently (and embarrassingly) they do it better. So if the Big Three want reciprocal success over there, they must forget forced entry into the market by politicians. Their goal must be to achieve the same local market effectiveness. In the long haul you only win if the customer is comfortable with the process and wants the product.

So, I'm going to fix all that when I'm President. Also, when I'm in the Oval Office, sun-dried tomatoes will be classified as illegal substances. I lived most of my life happily without them; suddenly it seems they are on, in, or with everything that is available for me to eat. I have no idea where they came from, but sometime in January 2013, on the day after my inauguration, they will be history. Then I'll attempt welfare reform.

# 6

## On Hurdling
## Marketplace Barriers

S trange. Despite all my glorious Olympic triumphs and gold medals, the moment that most people recall from my legendary athletic career was one of failure.[1] Back in the 1950s the world watched with bated breath as Roger Bannister and I were locked in combat, as only two immortal athletes could be, to see who would be first to break the four-minute-mile barrier. Mano a mano, indeed.

History records that it was he who swept past me down the final straight on the Oxford University running track on that cool English spring day in 1954, and the final great athletic barrier (more mental than physical?) was history. I lost, but was proud I had given my all. Perhaps if I had been able to benefit from modern training and nutritional programs it would have been different. (My diary notes indicate that during the evening before the great race I consumed seventeen pint glasses of foaming English ale along with at least two portions of a vindaloo curry sauce containing what the waiter insisted was chicken.) But all that would be pure conjecture.

---

[1]Thankfully, I had many triumphs. It was I, of course, who invented the Fosbury Flop long before Dick Fosbury came along and reinvented the high jump. Unfortunately, I invented it as part of the run-up to the javelin throw, and it never caught on.

After I moved from athletics to become a Captain of Industry, it often occurred to me that I had simply switched arenas, for there are many parallels in sport and business.[2] There are particular similarities between progressing in a competitive marketplace and journeying around a 400-meter track in pursuit of success.

On the surface, the best analogy is a hurdle race. There are relatively easy flat bits and then suddenly, out of the blue, you are forced to change your rhythm and technique completely and leap into the air. The idea, of course, is to miss the hurdle and land steadily, both feats achieved with such a level of skill that the rate of your forward progress barely slows. Few wise business managers put their game plans together without trying to figure out what the hurdles will be, when they will occur, and what will be needed to surmount them. But athletic hurdling can be a dangerous analogy for business as well as a helpful one. There are a number of profound differences to consider.

**Universal Law #31**

*As an athlete you might be thinking about 400-meter hurdles; as a businessperson you are thinking about a double marathon with steeplechase barriers.*

First, the longest hurdle race in athletics is the 3000-meter steeplechase and the second longest is only 400 meters. These are essentially short and middle distances for the athlete; but business needs to consider a marathon (or even longer). In reality the business race never ends, so you need a game plan for a double marathon with hurdles in it, which gives you some idea of the combined stamina and skill that have been endemic in the companies that have enjoyed long-term business success. Without exception, these companies have met and crossed many hurdles that

---

[2]Many is the time I've looked down a boardroom table and wanted to inspire my (executive) team with some of the poetry and rhetoric handed on to me by my old soccer coach. When things weren't going right early on in a game and we (the team) thought he'd be mad at us when we went in for the halftime break, he would often surprise us by staying calm and then sending us back out armed with (and motivated by) one of his simple, homespun philosophies, such as: "This isn't complicated, lads. Just kick the bastards."

have been placed in their way, although the popular conception is that they've just ground out a flat race over the years.

Disney is a classic example of this: Having grown dramatically in the thirties and forties as a Hollywood-based animated movie specialist company, they realized that their game plan had to address three big postwar market hurdles: the growth of television, the advent of mass travel and tourism, and the birth of more than 70 million babies in the U.S. between 1946 and 1964. Just carrying on doing what they were doing would not have allowed Disney to leap all these hurdles and keep their forward momentum going. In 1954 they became the first Hollywood name to embrace TV, through a long-term deal with ABC. Around the same time, Walt Disney poured his life savings into developing sixty acres of orange groves he had acquired near Anaheim, twenty-five miles south of Los Angeles. He had ideas for a Mickey Mouse park but as he said at the time, "It was hard for anybody to visualize what I had in mind." Cynics way outnumbered interested backers, but Disney built it and the theme park was born. All three hurdles were cleared.[3]

Coca-Cola is another company that has been running, and winning, the hurdle race for a century. Again, its progress has been so speedy and consistent it seems almost insulting to imply it has cleared barriers on the way. But it has, and plenty of them. The original development of bottled product, then fountain syrups, aluminum cans, international expansion, and the launch of Diet Coke (among many others) are all examples of hurdle leaping that kept Coca-Cola's momentum going when others tripped up. Yeah, the company clipped a few hurdles on the way (New Coke?), but it recovered and still leads its race.

There is a tendency (and an increasing modern pressure) to identify the business hurdle race as a sprint, understandably so when it seems corporate survival itself can depend on the next quarter's earnings. I watched recently as a CNN journalist calmly reported the dramatic slump of a high-tech, proprietary NASDAQ stock on the news of an earnings downgrade that effectively

---

[3]Disney is an example of a weird paradox in my personal thinking: I bow to no one in my respect for the management of the brand and the business concept, but I remain profoundly uncomfortable with many of their products.

halved the market value of the company. I suspect the white-faced CEO would have been singularly unimpressed with the idea that he should also have been concerned, that very evening, about hurdles coming up six months from then, let alone years down the track. But the great corporations manage it. Somehow.

The second big difference between athletic hurdling and business is that in athletics the hurdles are a set height and at set intervals. Most competent hurdlers, if they wanted to, could run their races blindfolded because they have a fixed stride pattern and hurdling technique. "Aha!" says the diligent student, busily taking notes (I can dream), "the issue here is *predictability*. In athletics the hurdles are stretching but predictable; in business they are stretching but not predictable. Vive la difference!" Well, yes and no.... The hurdles can be predictable in business, but not necessarily in conventional ways.

**Universal Law #32**

*If you are a facilities-based retailer and doing well, plan to be in the toilet within a year. If you are not doing well, you are already in it.*

Take retailing as an example, an industry I have been involved with for nearly thirty years on both sides of the Atlantic. After years of not recognizing the blindingly obvious, I have just developed my own universal theory for the science of facility-based retailing (i.e., you operate from a facility—a shop, kiosk, etc.): If you're not in the toilet now, you will be shortly. Retailing has such a low cost of entry; the important consumer variables (price, product, and service) are so dynamic that you can change any or all of them daily; and the consumers are so fickle that (if you're having a real good time as a retailer) you can plan on somebody's crashing your party. That applies at the corporate level and on the street, and it is before you contemplate the potential effects of non-facility-based retailing (direct marketing, catalog sales, the Internet, etc.). So if you are a retailer, you can predict hurdles even if you don't know what they look like. The winning game plans involve lightning-quick market responses and

the relentless pursuit of an understanding of the customer's mind-set. To predict the kind of hurdles you'll face, you need to think and act like a new entrant in your own business sector, which is how Sears has recovered the fumble against Wal-Mart.[4]

Some hurdles in business are predictable, but the difference is that there is usually no pattern. When you've just landed over one, you may face another immediately—there's no guarantee of a nice flat stretch. You may have a series of hurdles that are three feet tall, then one that is six feet high with water on the other side. Strangely enough, if the hurdles are predictable and regular, they become harder and not easier to handle. Gordon Moore (the cofounder of Intel) predicted in his famous Moore's Law that "the power and the complexity of the silicon chip will double every eighteen months." The general acceptance of that has meant the effort needed to stay ahead of the market is humongous. As a result Intel operates virtually as a research institution, plowing well over $1 billion a year into R&D. This, in turn, led to Andy Groves' corollary law: "Only the paranoid survive." The message is clear: If marketplace hurdles are in any way predictable, there can be no such thing as cruise control.

The third difference between hurdles in business and those in a foot race seems the hardest for business to grasp. The biggest and best have gotten this one wrong.

---

[4]Assuming one day Sears fixes its credit card business problems. For some reason I view retailers being in the credit business in the same way I would view Ben and Jerry's handling breast implants.

When an athlete hurdles, he or she takes off for the jump dressed (usually) in a form-fitting uniform and running shoes provided by the one of the world's newest religions (Nike or somesuch). He or she lands a split second later and (not surprisingly) still looks the same. That doesn't work in the hurdle race of business; in fact, it's a recipe for failure.

In business, when you land on the other side of your hurdle, *you must look different*. After a relatively easy start in the mid 1950s and on into the 1960s, Burger King reached its first market hurdle (slowing sales growth) and jumped. It landed on the other side of this hurdle wearing a new drive-through window on the side of the restaurant. The same pattern then repeated itself (good, but then slowing, sales growth), and the company jumped again. This time it came down open for breakfast with an appropriate new morning menu. And so on and so on. When I joined at the end of the eighties Burger King had to jump again, and this time it came down attracting families and kids, whereas before it had concentrated on the "blue collar male" niche, leaving the family market to McDonald's. In 1994 Burger King jumped up in the air with a Whopper, fries, and a drink costing up to $5, and came down with the whole menu restructured around $2.99 Value Meals.

**Universal Law #35**

*If you land on the other side of the market hurdle looking the same as you did when you approached it, you are probably heading for a SMEF (Spontaneous Massive Existence Failure).*

Another example of a company that survived almost certain death by leaping a hurdle and coming down looking profoundly different was Harley Davidson. By 1981 the Japanese threat had begun to pervade the heavy bike market, and HD was actually losing money. It had to leap this hurdle, but to come down looking the same would have merely postponed what Terry Jones (of Monty Python fame) has magnificently christened a SMEF (Spontaneous Massive Existence Failure) for the company. Underinvestment, poor processes, and inadequate management had left HD with an appalling quality reputation and an uneconomic manufacturing base. After a management buyout, the company landed on the other side of the hurdle and dramatically changed every aspect of the way it did business, introducing just-in-time (JIT) inventory techniques, employee involvement (EI), and a move away from traditional assembly line techniques with statistical operator control (SOC). It added to that a revolutionary marketing concept (the HOG, Harley Owners' Groups), added a further teaspoon of protectionism by the U.S. government, and rewrote its history. This example fascinates me: The company saw the Japanese as a hurdle, ran at it, jumped up in the air looking like Harley Davidson, and came down on the other side looking more like the hurdle than the hurdle.

Who *didn't* figure this concept out? IBM was probably the best-equipped and fastest athlete in the computer-world hurdle race of the 1960s and 1970s. As the science of computing enabled more mass data to be processed dramatically more quickly, in fewer mysterious blue fridges kept in air-conditioned rooms somewhere behind the accounting department, IBM looked unstoppable. Then in the eighties up came a hurdle. IBM jumped, and came down looking exactly the same. Disaster. That particular marketplace hurdle represented a sea change in the science, with an irrevocable shift away from centralized data processing to distributed applications and personal computing. Even companies like Digital misread it, figuring that outbased terminals connected to minicomputers would do the trick. But Apple cleared this hurdle and came down recognizing that computing was now about consumer branding and hired a marketing guy from Pepsi to run the company for a while. Microsoft figured the way to interplanetary domination was to develop an operating system to help the newly enfranchised public work that bloodythingwiththescreen they rashly bought using their Visa card after a heavy holiday party lunch.

When I say IBM experienced disaster, I mean *disaster*. IBM wiped some $70 billion[5] (yes, billion) off its market value in the late eighties as it well and truly tripped on this hurdle try-

[5]I'm fifty years old as I write this. I remember when $1 billion was a lot of money. This was, of course, before our two sons arrived at their late teenage years.

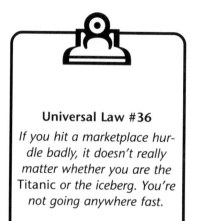

ing to clear it. It jumped into the air looking like the *Titanic* and came down looking like the iceberg. Now, there's a trick.

Just to prove Hegel's famous point (that we don't learn from history), both the winners shot themselves in the feet on the next lap. Didn't the world mourn as the arrogant, unassailable Microsoft cheerfully entered the Guinness Book of Misjudgments in its own right in the mid 1990s? In 1995 it launched Windows 95 with roughly the profile of a mid-size European war and a marketing budget the size of India's GNP. There was a market hurdle in front of the company, sure enough, but it jumped up as Windows and came down as (a bit more fancy) Windows. It should have come down recognizing that operating systems had moved on from providing the ability to perform miracles at your own work station to providing access to cyberspace and a zillion other work stations. Planet Earth sent a clear message to Microsoft: Modems have arrived!

All of a sudden it was Microsoft who looked like it had built the world's heaviest airplane (which was Bill Gate's derisory description of 1980s IBM) or, using my analogy, it took over as the biggest thing built for the wrong reason since the Egyptian pyramids.

Both Big Blue and Bill Gates have figured it all out now and are back in the race, but not everyone has the resources to recover from that kind of stumble. The universal law is clear: Look different when you land.

The last difference between an Olympic hurdle race and business is good news for the latter: Unlike the athlete, the businessperson doesn't always have to go over the barrier. You can go around or (occasionally) under them. In late 1994, the magazine *Auto Rental News* shook that industry (and a few onlookers) by naming the St. Louis–based Enterprise Rent-A-Car Co. number one in the U.S., ticking off Hertz enormously by so doing.[6] Measuring by size of fleet (Enterprise's 232,000 vs. Hertz's 215,000) and number of office locations (2000 vs. 1175), the magazine had a case; but whatever the criteria used, many were surprised that this no-name brand was even close to the well-known giant. In truth, comparisons are irrelevant: The two companies barely compete with each other. While Hertz, Avis, and Alamo duke it out at the airports for business and leisure travelers, Enterprise concentrates on the suburban insurance replacement market. Given the clutter and competitive economics of the business and leisure markets, it proved a master strategy for Enterprise to simply walk around the sides of all those hurdles and (effectively) run on a parallel track.

After all that, I don't suppose any of you are interested in my much-heralded performance in the recent Olympics where, unfortunately, I could only come up with another silver medal. This time it was not surprising as, in the outdoor heat of the Olympic pool in Atlanta, two of us from Britain took on the hottest of hot favorites in one of the newly recognized sports. History records we lost by a wide margin to (the favorites) France in the finals for synchronized surrendering. Not interested? I didn't think you would be.

---

[6]This occasion gave birth to some memorable trade journalism, of the "It only Hertz when Enterprise laughs" variety.

# 7

## On Unhealthy Profit

I would have preferred that it had been withheld from the public, but it seems that everybody now knows that in the mid 1990s I rejected Louis Farrakhan's invitation to address his historic Million Man March in Washington. D.C. My reasoning was simple: In these hard times a guy's got to earn a living and I told him that if he was expecting a million men, I'd do the gig for a dollar a head. Cash up front.

His backers just couldn't put the deal together and he was devastated. He so wanted me to speak from the vantage point of one of the most oppressed groups on the planet—white, male, ex-CEOs of Burger King Corp.

No worries. Let me tell you about another Million Person March (this time women will be invited) coming up soon, at which I will definitely speak. Pro bono.

We are all going to protest against the myopic, paranoid, stupid pursuit of *unhealthy* corporate earnings, which to some degree covers (my estimation) up to a third of the declared profits of Western business. During the ceremonies I expect to be awarded the Lifetime Achievement Award for Hypocrisy[1] because (on reflection) I've committed my fair share of this crime against humanity.

---

[1] I'm by no means a shoo-in. Competition is fierce, with the final nominees including Pope John Paul the Bestseller, the head of the Whitewater investigation (now in its twenty-seventh year), and Queen Elizabeth the Second (now better known, of course, as Diana's mother-in-law).

If I had my life to live again (or could choose a reincarnation model), I'd be the first son of the Sultan of Brunei. Second choice would be a guru, writer, or commentator on business. In that position, without actually having run a big company, you can yell at your audience (Tom Peters), pontificate (Peter Drucker), gently ruminate (Charles Handy), or mislead and confuse them (Hammer and Champy). This is a tough chapter for me, as it would be for anyone (I repeat: anyone) who has had profit responsibility for a big hunk of a public company. We have all been guilty of a degree of padding the earnings figure to meet or beat expectations. I do not want this treatise to be a mea culpa (although there are some places where I would like to rub a mental vanishing cream on my memory). The intent is to highlight the difficulties of running a business in the glare of the market makers' searchlights. We will observe some universal laws to support the quality of declared earnings when under such pressure in a way that conventional auditing refuses to.

My observation is that there are five practices (they are by no means mutually exclusive) that threaten the quality of profits: the absolute focus on managing the bottom line and not the business; milking the customer through myopic pricing; supporting the weak soldier in the corporate platoon; crash-diet cost cutting; and the manipulation of the discretionary cost cycle of the business.

GrandMet (the U.K. multinational I worked for) had quite an astonishing variety of businesses for ten years from the mid 1980s (particularly at the start of that period). They ranged from alcoholic drinks to food products, chewing tobacco to eye care, branded restaurants to pubs, ice cream to off-track betting, but they all had one thing in common: The senior management of the different companies managed earnings as a priority, not the businesses or the markets. Now, here's the contentious bit: It was no big deal. I was one of those guys, and I worked with a bunch of excellent businessmen and women. We had a tremendous record in brand building[2] and aggressive international

---

[2]Most of it intentional, although rumor has it that the birth of Bailey's Irish Cream liqueur came about when someone at one of our dairy operations in Ireland spilled his lunch (one bottle of Irish whiskey) into the 2,000,000-gallon vat of milk he was supervising. Sounds about right....

growth. Allen Sheppard (now Lord Didgemere) was a hero of mine then and is a hero of mine now. (I'd like to be quite clear on this because the mouthbreathers in the "City" consider him an acquired taste.) He led us in a philosophy that the end, to which all our efforts were means, was earnings per share growth. If we delivered our short-term profit goals, "the long-term profit performance would take care of itself." It was assumed you would have an arm-wrestle with the auditors at the year's end, but it was also assumed you would stay within the rules, you would behave with towering integrity, you would build brand equity, and you would treat all your people and partners (winners and losers) with fairness and respect. In hindsight, among a thousand good things, we did some dumb ones to support short-term earnings that (probably) caused us more problems in the medium term than they solved in the short.

I define *dumb*, when managing the bottom line of the business, as not illegal, malicious, or materially deceptive. When those kinds of practices enter the realms a company can move from needing outpatient treatment to requiring intensive care.

There's a spectrum of behavior involved here with no one at either extreme end, but an example of being as close to the wrong end as you wannabe highlights the potential dire implications. In 1995, *Business Week* magazine did a fine job of open-heart surgery on Bausch and Lomb, the parent company of a bunch of fine products and brands including Ray-Ban sunglasses. The investigation looked under the surface of the company's audited results for the previous two years, and the first thing to note of interest is that it took six months of prying to uncover what was going on (remember, this is a public company). Some fifty interviews with current and former employees later, we found out what "manage the bottom line" can really mean when it is supported by demented, paranoid management. This outfit found itself caught in the self-made trap of pursuing the goal of double-digit earnings growth that was announced, and pretty much committed to, before the start of each year.

Led by Chairman and CEO Daniel E. Gill,[3] the corporate culture was simple: Your targets were handed down at the start of the year and you delivered them or died. Nothing unusual here: Despite the rhetoric in Western business about "agreeing on" goals, most of them involve a top-down process of one kind or another, but most companies then have checks and balances in place to stop pure anarchy from prevailing. B&L is an example of what can happen when you don't. Among the better examples: In its Pacific region it inflated revenues by faking sales of sunglasses to real customers and booking the sales at year end, then followed this up by factoring receivables and dumping products that the customers refused. The contact lens managers shipped products that doctors never ordered and forced distributors to take up to two years' worth of unwanted inventories. Every Red Ball day (the last day of an accounting period) would find panic-stricken managers discounting drastically or extending credit. Savvy customers waited till the end of the period to get the best deals (often ordering on a Saturday), and sometimes as much as 70 percent of a month's goods were shipped in the last three days. Eventually the whole thing imploded, and during the catch-up and clean-up period B&L's earnings dropped 54 percent and the stock price fell to $30 from a high of $60. Virtually the whole senior management team has been replaced, including Gill—who sadly had to leave his three jets, multimillion dollar compensation, and new $70 million office block behind (all funded by this crap act; pass the sick bag, Alice).

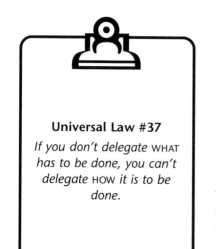

**Universal Law #37**

If you don't delegate WHAT has to be done, you can't delegate HOW it is to be done.

This brings us to our first universal law: The less you delegate what is to be done in the short term (i.e., you impose business targets rather than agree on them), the less you can delegate how they are achieved. You have to

---

[3]This guy would surely finish in the top three should *Fortune* ever produce a list of capitalism's 500 all time greatest donkey-wallopers.

install checks and balances (particularly at year end) on the practices behind the figures, and you must have countervailing forces (e.g., compensation based on quality, long-term goals, etc.).

Another form of unhealthy profit can come from companies with the most virtuous of management, but who misread their markets and misprice their products or services. The most common sin here is what Drucker calls "the worship of high profit margins and premium pricing." He cites the near-collapse of Xerox in the 1970s as a prime example of what can happen to a company that gets this wrong. Having invented the copier, they began to add feature after feature, each priced to yield maximum profit margin and each driving up the machine's price. Result? Japan's Canon entered the market with a simple machine, and Xerox barely survived.

Mispricing was an epidemic in Burger King at the end of the 1980s, partly because of the idiotic cost-plus pricing approach that is so prevalent in the food service business, but also partly because the company responded to a problem in a way that is so stupid you really couldn't make it up. For a whole variety of reasons, sales were in decline at the time, and a standard franchisee response to this lower revenue challenge was to raise prices (!).[4] You'll agree this is pure gold, and just why the customers didn't respond with waves of enthusiasm to this master tactic is beyond me. Astonishingly, the way they did respond to higher prices was to visit the restaurant less and buy less when they did come. Which lowered the same store's sales again. Now what could the operators do? I know, put prices up again....

Pure cost-plus pricing is another sinner here, and the reason why America and Britain no longer have a consumer electronics industry. Again, good old Burger King gave us a case study in how not to do this at the end of the eighties when it was deemed a heinous crime to suggest dropping the gross percent-

---

[4]Other tactics chosen to respond to the drop-off in customers: Cut restaurant wages (i.e., reduce service standards further), cut cosmetic maintenance (i.e., make the restaurant look worse), and cut investment promotions (i.e., give the customer less incentive to come). All in all, Daniel Gill would have been proud....

age (GP) profit on any single item below an arbitrary minimum. The logic of selling three at 60 percent markup as against two at 65 percent simply would not hold water with a franchisee's strange math, and changes only came about when sales tanked drastically and the concept of combo margin pricing was introduced. Any mispricing above what the market is willing to pay, for whatever reason, will support earnings only for a short period and is unhealthy for the medium and long terms. It will invariably create a market for a competitor (Taco Bell came hurtling into the overpriced fast food market in the early nineties) or reduce sales or repeat purchases. Customers do not give a rat's ass about your cost structure or the math of your margin calculations or your own view of your brand equity. They care about their value perception, and price-led costing (not vice versa) is the only model that is healthy and sustainable.

On to one of my favorites: When earnings are under pressure, what better than a dramatic, overnight reduction in costs (a.k.a. downsizing, reengineering, or the corporate crash diet)? This is obviously much easier than seeking a hike in revenues, and so much more effective: Maybe only 10 to 20 percent of increased sales will hit the bottom line, but 100 percent of real cost savings will do so. Take a big restructuring charge and, with a bit of creative accounting, you can underpin earnings for a couple of years. Then it will be time for another restructuring. This practice has almost become what bloodletting was to the medieval physician—the cure for every illness. Hundreds, thousands of companies out there are trying to figure out ways to eat their seed corn as slowly as possible, but case study after case study are now indicating that the health of these profit-improved companies is far from guaranteed.

In the first place there is evidence that many of the trumpeted profit improvements fail to come through. A mid 1990s survey by the American Management Association (AMA) found that fewer than half the companies that had downsized since 1990 went on to report higher operating profits in the years following the move, and even fewer saw improved productivity.

From my own experience most of the corporate weight lost in these crash diets goes back on fast, either through creep-back recruitment (*somebody* has to do the work) or indirectly through expensive outsourcing. More to the point, however, is the health price you can pay if you do increase profitability in the short term. Two *Economist* case studies (April 1996) illustrate the point for Nynex (the U.S. regional telephone group) and Delta Airlines. Both downsized dramatically, with unhealthy results for both: Delta lost its clear service edge (and a lot of customer loyalty)

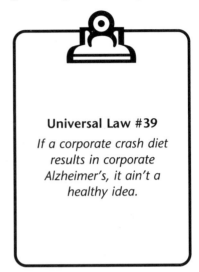

**Universal Law #39**

*If a corporate crash diet results in corporate Alzheimer's, it ain't a healthy idea.*

and Nynex ended up paying customers a rebate for a slump in service standards. A crash diet can support this year's earnings, but can bring on symptoms of what John Challenger (Challenger, Gray and Christmas, Chicago consultants) calls "corporate Alzheimer's"—the permanent loss of a firm's skills, knowledge, collective business experience, culture, vision, and numerous other intangible qualities. It's what the Japanese call tacit knowledge—hunches, know-how, ideals, and experience— and the profit improvement that throws that away ain't always healthy.

Now here's one from my own case book that I guess is prevalent in the kind of business structure I've worked in: big corporations with (relatively) autonomous operating companies that are consolidated for accounting purposes at a center. Here, often with your targets agreed to and performance on track, you can fall victim to the need to support the weak soldier in the corporate platoon. In the early 1990s Burger King was really waking up; we were poised for a good year and looking solid beyond that. Then, with about two months to go in the financial year, Pillsbury (also owned by the same parent, GrandMet) signaled a disaster and came off its year-end forecast. The message came out that we had a multimillion-dollar problem (at GrandMet level) against analyst's expectations. What could we "contribute"? The answer was that we (in Burger King) could contribute a lot, and a lot more and a lot faster than anyone else in the group because we had a unique process that could generate big profits fast. It meant we sold a bunch of high-performing company-run restaurants at fire sale prices to franchisees, closing the sales within the financial year. On each sale we'd book a profit on the sale of the asset, but would lose the retail income from then on. Sure, we booked a big profit number that year (and helped solve the overall corporate problem), but was it healthy? Nah. Not only did it inflate our profitability in the current year to unreal, unsustainable levels, it meant we had to top that next year to show continuing growth, but on a trading base with fewer company restaurants. So what happens then? You sell more restaurants in the next year to bridge the gap, and suddenly a company that was balanced is out of the pocket and scrambling.

**Universal Law #40**

*If you have a weak soldier in the corporate platoon, do not jeopardize the health of the others by asking them for support. The weak either recover on their own or get left behind (a.k.a. sold).*

Clearly, we did the wrong thing for the right reason. GrandMet got through its year end and we helped the weak soldiers, as I'm sure they would have helped us in reverse circumstances. But it stank. I wasn't happy about it then, I'm not happy about it on reflection, and I'm sure we broke a universal rule, the one invented by Darwin: If you have a weak performer in the portfolio, let it die off or recover on its own. Don't jeopardize the health of the healthy by bailing it out.

The last route to unhealthy profit is now almost a science and is so prevalent in most corporations it is hardly noticed. Every company has a base of fixed costs (which you can't effect within, say, a year) and a range of variable ones on top (which you can almost turn on and off like a tap). There is a huge range of the latter—marketing, travel and entertainment, maintenance, contract labor, filling vacancies, meeting expenses, etc.—and what happens in many companies is a watered-down version of the Bausch and Lomb syndrome: As you approach the year's end and feel the need to secure your forecast figures, all discretionary spending gets put on hold.

Depending on how you view the risk, this hold can vary from a couple of weeks (perfectly normal) to eleven months (extreme). Again, depending on the risk it can range from a cutback in travel and entertainment (T&E) and a delay in filling vacancies (perfectly normal) to a complete ban on all maintenance expenses, a laying off of all contractors, abandonment of all marketing support programs, a complete T&E freeze, and a closedown of the telephone system (extreme). What happens then is that the pent-up demand for these expenses has to be met when the new year's budgets are released, and expenditures then zoom to crazy heights, before the panic sets in again and we repeat the process at the end of the following year, maybe for a teeny bit longer and involving a few more activities.

Douglas Adams (*The Hitchhiker's Guide to the Galaxy*) once described planet Earth as "mostly harmless" and so, frankly, is most of this kind of activity. But beware: This behavior can become a habit. Profits that are supported like this once have a way of becoming reliant on such behavior. And it is addictive: What starts as trivial and commonsense rapidly becomes material and stupid, and once you get in the cycle you can't find a way out. The universal rule is: Keep it under control. If your discretionary costs are more than 50 percent lower in the last two months of the corporate year than they are in the first two, that is a symptom of a disease. Stop and fix the disease, whatever it takes.

**Universal Law #41**

*If the level of your discretionary costs is more than 50 percent lower in the last two months of the year than in the first two, that is the symptom of a disease. Stop and fix the disease.*

All these practices produce unhealthy profit and therefore potentially mislead investors and everybody else with a vested interest. Although examples of the Bausch and Lomb kind are rare, at the other end of the spectrum these practices are commonplace, and few companies would escape deep scrutiny. Indeed, Ian Griffiths, city editor of London's influential evening paper, rolls the following grenade down the table in his book[5]:

> "Every Company is fiddling its profits. Every set of accounts is based on books which have been gently cooked, or completely roasted."

**Universal Law #42**

*Good results are the end product of good business activities over a period. They may be high or low in numeric terms (just like bad results).*

On reflection—deep reflection—I'm in his camp. I have spent a lot of my career in this kitchen, although I would claim to be the gentlest of cooks. It sure is a crowded kitchen, though.

When, oh, when will Western business and capitalism realize earnings are an *end result* of a series of business activities over a period of time? Good results are the end product of a series of good business activities over that period, and they may be high or low in numeric terms. Bad results are the result of bad business, and here's the weird bit: *They can be just as high or low.*

Even the best companies get sucked into doing the most stupid things. Rubbermaid, for example, has a tremendous reputation and a solid, distinct position in a marketplace that is a sea of commodity products. A while ago, fueled by prestated U.S. earnings ambitions that started going wrong midyear, they started drinking stupid juice and dumped heavily discounted products on a customer at the year's end to boost revenues for the period. Trouble was, Wal-Mart (who just happened to be another customer of theirs) got to hear of the higher discounts and went bananas (that's a technical term procurement managers use to describe a state of

---

[5]Ian Griffiths, *New Creative Accounting* (MacMillan, 1992).

extreme unhappiness). Result? Rubbermaid lost shelf space in Wal-Mart. Brilliant.

Stockholders are the lifeblood of limited liability capitalism. Question: Am I happy as a stockholder in Rubbermaid with a couple of points higher earnings growth achieved at the cost of fracturing relationships with the biggest retailer in the U.S.?

We can't look to the auditing profession to help us here. In theory, auditors are employed by the owners of businesses (the stockholders) for their protection, and to a degree this is achieved. Auditors will yell like hell if a company tries to depreciate its truck fleet over too long a period of time or if it is untimely with bank reconciliations. What auditors will not tell you is that results have been achieved by a series of misguided, myopic, damaging activities as long as those activities are legal by their definition or outside the scope of the audit. So we must look to ourselves—enlightened (and in my case sadder and wiser) capitalists—for answers.

So that's what we're going to protest in my Million Person March, scheduled for my birthday next year. I have agreed with local police it will start at Botticelli Trattoria in Coral Gables, Miami, and proceed several yards to John Martin's Irish Bar. We will conclude with the singing of the first part of America's corporate hymn:

> Jesus, help me through next quarter,
> I need profits like a rock.
> If I don't make what I oughtta,
> Christ, I'll have to dump some stock!

(Chorus)    *I have frozen all expenses,*
*Air travel now is totally banned.*
*Marketing costs are all past tenses,*
*But earnings will come in as planned.*

# 8

## On Making Decisions
## (and Staying Out of Jail)

I went to see the Disney movie *Pocahontas* for one reason and one reason only: to see with my own eyes if the rumor was true. It was. The male native Americans (or the "Indians" as they were known in the countless western movies and comic books of my youth) have no nipples, and it was at this juncture I realized that big-business capitalism—as I had known it and as it had attracted me for a career—was over. I left it shortly afterward.

I'd seen the signs before, of course, but just not realized how bad it was. Early in the nineties (and here I must confess to a life of poor judgement in picking my drinking partners) I was in Europe when Boris Yeltsin called me and suggested we have a boy's night out together, celebrating his recent recovery from a quintuple[1] heart bypass. He'd come across some of my writing in the sanatorium waiting room. (Author's note: That might have been an article I wrote on Business Strategy for *Yeeehaaa!*, the in-house weekly for the Wisconsin Militia.[2])

[1] I think it was quintuple. I may be wrong by two or three.

[2] Total circulation: seventeen, but this did not count wives, cousins, sisters, etc. Sometimes one person was all of these.

Anyway, Boris and I met in Berlin and, boy, did we blitz it. The man drank like a rhino and left me way behind as he got himself outside several bottles of a potent wood alcohol he had especially imported from the hills behind Galway Bay in Ireland.[3] Purely medicinal, he assured me—its purpose was to thin out the blood. Wow.

With slurred speech, Boris told me of his admiration for my chronicles and said he was seeking help with something that was confusing him. Why wasn't capitalism working for the old Soviet bloc? Real evidence was emerging that the long-awaited freedom of choice for the oppressed population of the U.S.S.R. was leading to a steady return to Communism and regulation via the electoral box.

I swished the little plastic umbrella about in my drink.[4] My reply held little comfort for either of us. I told him that I was losing faith in Western capitalism and that there were thousands like me. The key to our frustration lay in the inability, imposed or self-imposed, of Western business leadership to make a decision that was timely, properly thought through, free of static interference from extraneous forces, and balanced. In essence, the ability to do all those had seen capitalism historically prosper as the best social and economic system. Those principles were at the heart of Adam Smith's Invisible Hand theory and were the force behind all progress in free market enterprise: the pursuit of vested self-interest.

Three countering forces have emerged in the last quarter-century that have all but stopped the flow of good commercial decision making: the arrival of a demented legal profession; the increasingly high (and frequently fatal) price of making an error; and the ability, in the information age, to research and analyze options for so long that you never actually make the decision. I'll deal with them in the reverse order to which they attract me: Lawyers first.

---

[3]This has astonishing properties, one of which is to enable the drinker, after just a few glasses, to compose sentimental Irish ballads and sing them at the same time.

[4]To see if I could prevent its dissolving.

The control of business decision making by lawyers is a U.S.-led phenomenon. A country that has 5 percent of the world's population and 66 percent of the world's lawyers couldn't do anything but lead the charge, and I became acutely aware of it on my second day in the U.S., when I arrived to run Burger King. How I missed it on my first, I shall never know.

It has always been important to me, in whatever management position I have held, to respond personally to mail and phone calls addressed to me. It was not always possible if I was traveling and a quick response was needed or if somebody else could (frankly) respond more effectively. But it was (and still is) important to me to give it my best shot. Just as Sam Walton used store visits as a way of keeping his finger on the pulse of his business, part of my modus operandi was to listen and respond to anybody—customer, vendor, analyst, critic (whoever)—who took the personal trouble to write or phone. Frankly, it was an enjoyable part of my business mix.[5]

At the end of the second day at Burger King, I had a pile, and I mean a *pile,* of such correspondence waiting to be dealt with and was explaining to my assistant that my method was to scribble short replies in the margins of the actual incoming letter and mumble the longer ones into a dictaphone.[6] We were interrupted by a smart young man who came in, nervously picked up my pile of mail, and made to leave. He was from our legal department and it was (apparently) his job to answer (or get answered) all the CEO's mail. The consequences of a nonlegal mind doing it were deemed to be of potential Titanic-like proportions. I took a deep breath and sprung a leak (the first of many, so I made sure it was a good one; I knew it would be the topic of much discussion). When I lose my temper, I lose it, just as when I laugh I let everybody in the same zip code know I'm

[5]I received some wonderful letters at Burger King that probably justify a book on their own. One asked me, "How many hamburgers do you get out of a cow?" The answer was, of course, that we didn't know. We started in 1954 and this was (I think) in 1992. We hadn't finished the first one yet....

[6]Serious point: This conversation took place in 1989, a decade ago. Doesn't dictating seem primitive with the advent of E-mail and PCs? I wonder if any executives still dictate out there? Shame on you if you do.

**Universal Law #43**

*If you are a leader, show your emotional involvement. If you lose your temper, get the decibel level up to that of a* Who *concert. When you laugh, light up the entire zip code.*

amused. I'm in the camp that believes leaders should show emotional involvement with what's going on around them and, despite the fact it's got nothing to do with this chapter, I'm going to make it a universal law. Because it's my book, I'm doing it right here.

I left my man in no doubt that I would be handling my own in-tray in the future and that I would occasionally seek advice from him, as I would from anybody else in the business if I thought it relevant. Would you believe the bastards then invented a scheme to kidnap my out-tray as a second line of defense? I had to come up with a counterploy to kill this plan as well. I waited until a suitable letter arrived, and it was a beauty. I couldn't make this up if I tried, but someone wrote in and complained that, after recently eating a Whopper (hamburger), he developed a nasty boil that moved (remember I'm not inventing this) and finally located itself at the base of his scrotum. It caused him great agony before it finally burst (He enclosed bed linen samples as evidence, both to me and to his local health authority!) and he asked if I would care to compensate him financially before he referred the matter to his attorney. I'd get twenty letters a day like this, shooting for a quick $5,000 payoff, but this one was a jewel, so I drafted a reply. I wrote that after careful research, our labs had identified that his problem was unique: that he had been visited by Worstheimer's Traveling Boil, a malady that hadn't been reported in the U.S. in more than 150 years. Its only known cause was from eating moldy ship's biscuits, and I wondered if he'd been on an Alaskan cruise recently. I advised him that the only cure was to tape a piece of European blue cheese to his ankle and set his alarm clock for 2 A.M. When he woke up, the boil would have traveled to his ankle in response to the pungent smell, and he should then hit it with a copy of the Yellow Pages.

I enclosed a free Whopper coupon (!) and signed the letter, sending a copy to our legal department. I put the lawyer's copy in my out-tray, threw the actual outgoing letter away, and waited. The way our legal department eventually approached me to "contain the potential situation damage" would have scripted a Monty Python movie (and I'm still laughing as I type this), but I made my point. I would do the job I was paid to do, with their help and advice provided when appropriate. They would be like any other department, there to support the business with their special skills, but no more or no less than marketing, finance, product development, etc. As CEO, I would stand by my activities and decisions and be held accountable if they were wrong. What's more, if we had made a cartoon movie, our males would have had nipples.

Now it's time for me to backtrack a bit. My chief counsel was one of the most able executives I have ever worked with and many of his team were very capable. So are many lawyers I know professionally and personally. Half of my first college degree was in law (in a desperate attempt to get my overall grades up[7]), and a distant friend of mine once knew somebody who had a relative who married somebody who knew a lawyer. Apparently he was okay. What we're talking about is what happens when common sense and moderation exit the stage. If you run a business (or a unit or a team), here's a universal law to follow: If you were to produce a cartoon movie and your legal team would decide for you that the males would not have nipples, you are not running the business well, and they are running it badly.

**Universal Law #44**

*If your business were to produce a cartoon movie and your legal team would decide for you that the males would have no nipples, then you are not running the business well, and they are running it badly.*

Capitalism is a living, breathing, organism and its main arteries are slowly being clogged by the saturated fats of the Western legal profession.

[7]It worked. As my friend at the university magnificently put it: "All you have to do with law is put ten hours a day in for a couple of weeks prior to the exam, then vomit it all out on the day of the exam, and you get top marks." It worked for me.

It's all got to do with risk taking, two words that many argue are the best simple definition of capitalism. Risk taking can take many forms in business: a new venture, a product launch, an investment project, a marketing campaign, and so on. All of these have one common element: By definition, they can go wrong. Of course good management attempts to minimize risks, but nothing is risk-free in enterprise.

Lawyers and litigation have now made any wound received from making a wrong decision potentially fatal for a business and quite out of balance with any potential gains from these ventures. Mass tort and class actions can now threaten the very existence of a company years after risks were taken and accepted by all concerned, even risks that were framed within the knowledge base and body of litigation that existed at the time. To revisit responsibility in the light of new knowledge is to rewrite history. It's an ugly concept and one that will surely choke commercial risk taking.

One way this trend is damaging enterprise is by affecting the business of distributing products and services through agents. Franchising is a classic example (albeit only one of many): The franchisee seeks the benefit of somebody else's brand development skills, and the franchisor seeks the benefit of faster, broader, and cheaper brand distribution. Both parties benefit from the economies of scale in purchasing and marketing.

The franchisee remains an independent business in this model and, as such, is subject to the risks and vagaries of modern business fortune. Of course, a franchisee should be protected from bad practices by the franchisor (such as poor support for the brand); but what is happening is that the law is beginning to insist that the franchisor underwrite virtually *all* the risks of the franchisee. As a result franchising, which can be a real catalyst for economic growth (particularly in developing countries), may well become so unattractive to brand owners that it could disappear within twenty-five years. If Jim McLamore and Dave Edgerton were starting Burger King today, they would be crazy to contemplate franchising as a growth strategy.

Another of the lungs of capitalism is OPM—the use of Other People's Money to grow and develop businesses. It too is being affected by the legal cancer. New business start-ups (the lifeblood of free enterprise) depend on networks of investors prepared to take risks, on a limited liability basis, to provide the venture capital necessary to grow a business to adolescence. But limited liability itself is now under threat with entrepreneurs and their brokers now threatened with litigation when a new idea crashes and burns. Somebody please tell these particular lawyers—these smug, parasitic, modern-day warrior-poets who concentrate on attacking genesis companies—that this is *the basic idea of capitalism.* Ninety percent of new ideas fail on takeoff, and small investments are lost. This commercial Darwinism ensures that the winners are real winners, and small investments can generate lottery-style payouts. People who can't afford to lose shouldn't invest in high-risk start-ups; those are for a specific kind of investor only. If we choke the supply of new venture capital because of the sheer fear of the consequences of failing, we choke the very life out of capitalism.

Another specter now haunts effective and efficient decision making, one that is riddled with irony. In his remarkable study of the history of risk management, Peter Bernstein[8] argues that the notion of bringing risk under control when making decisions is one of the central ideas that distinguishes modern times from the more distant past. Although the basic principles of probability theory, game theory, sampling, regressing to the mean, trialing, and the Law of Great Numbers have been around for centuries, it is my observation that any graph that plotted our historic ability to perform all these analyses routinely and extensively would show exponential growth in the last twenty-five years.

Bernstein records the lifetime contributions of Jacob Bernoulli who, although he died in 1705, is spiritually alive and kicking in many large consultancies and corporate strategic planning departments today. In his infamous jar, Bernoulli had 5000 pebbles, of which 2000 were white and 3000 black. He surmised that if you drew them out one by one, carefully not-

---

[8]Peter Bernstein, *Against the Gods* (John Wiley and Sons, 1996).

ing the color of each one before putting it back, eventually you would be able to be pretty sure of the ratio between the two colors. In his estimation, after a mere 25,550 drawings you would be 98 percent sure of the right answer. Brilliant. As my contribution to history and upon all your behalves, I have played a game. I estimate it would take a day or so to draw 25,550 times, but (approximately) two hours to empty the little pebbles all over the carpet and *actually count them.*

The access to massive data banks, the advent of cyberspace, and the mind-boggling growth in electronic data processing power have put us all in a danger of becoming Bernoullis.[9] The essence of managing risk when making a decision is to maximize the areas where we have some control over the outcome while minimizing the areas where we don't. The problem is that modern science, coupled with an increasing fear of the consequences of getting it wrong, is enabling us (and tempting us) to prolong and extend the option analysis stage of decision making. Hang on a minute, let's just draw one more pebble before we finally decide.

A year or so ago I was in Europe working with an organization that brought together, in the loosest possible sense, a collection of individual accounting firms outside the Big Six. This was a real opportunity (maybe better defined as a real need) for them to work together across international borders to compete with the giants. I confess I was never at ease with accounting but, even to my uneducated mind, the areas of potential synergy were significant. In fairness, they had seen the possibilities, and this is how they had gone about making them happen: Two years previously they had started the debate about who should be on the committee to think about it. No real progress had been made and we dedicated our time together to really trying to close this one down. It was agreed that a formal nominating committee would now consider that issue for (another) year, and then come back with proposals as to who should be in the working party—the group that would then in

---

[9]It is one of my ambitions to bring Bernoulli into the English language, as in, "Will you stop Bernoulliing about on the side and get in the swimming pool?" or, "Can you call Strategic Planning for me and see if the Vice President of Bernoulliing is available?"

turn go away and look at the actual problems and opportunities. The timetable envisaged for the latter process? One to three years. Then, of course, a mechanism would have to be designed to make any actual decisions, at which time a jar filled with black and white pebbles would be issued.

What is happening here is a profound acceleration of what John Maynard Keynes identified as long ago as 1936: "Worldly wisdom teaches that it is better...to fail conventionally than to succeed unconventionally."[10] Leaders seem much happier with a process that researches the ass off an option and then trawls and trawls the available data in the hope that a conventional, sophisticated decision will eventually make itself, without any degree of impulse, judgment, or pragmatism. Won't work, though. So let's introduce the first double universal law: We don't want no tidy graveyards, and we would far rather have completely unexplainable success than sophisticated reasons for failure. Both the pace and the potential scope of market change mean you must bring all of the above into play. IBM recently woke up one morning suddenly facing a combined Compaq/DEC competitor. Delta woke up and found Continental had merged with Northwest Airlines. These companies can't commission a three-year study to tell them how to respond, nor can they run their massive computers for two years to analyze the new playing field. The reality is that even their computers aren't big enough now.

**Universal Law #45**

*When making decisions, remember: We don't want no tidy graveyards.*

**Universal Law #46**

*Completely unexplainable success is far preferable to sophisticated reasons for failure.*

[10]John Maynard Keynes, *The General Theory of Employment, Interest and Money* (Harcourt Brace, 1936).

**Universal Law #47**

*Get yourself quickly into a position where you are 80 percent confident you are right, then make the decision. Another two years of research will probably only move your confidence level to 83 percent.*

Business decision making needs two new universal laws, and I have world copyrights on both.[11] The first of these states (firmly) that you can quickly get yourself into a position where you are 80 percent sure you are right about a decision, and then take another two years moving that to 83 percent. The rule says to make the decision at the 80 percent stage and then fix it as you go. If it proves wrong, as it did in the cases of New Coke and McRib (and just about every other McDonald's new product launch of the 1990s), it is unlikely that the extra two years of desktop research would have revealed the fault line in your thinking. If you keep getting 'em wrong, of course, it indicates that from a purely executive point of view, you probably couldn't hit a cow's ass with a banjo.

**Universal Law #48**

*Even the most seminal decisions about your business strategy, vision, or whatever can and should be made by the right people, with the right summary information, locked away off site in a room with no chairs and no phones in it for three hours.*

The second is the three-hour law that applies to shaping business strategy. Even the most seminal decisions about your business strategy, vision, or direction (delete as applicable) can and should be made by the right people, with the right summary information, locked away off site in a room with no chairs and no phones in it for three hours. Try it for your business—the results will amaze you.

Although my observation is that it is rampant today, the aversion to taking risks that is driven by fear of failure or by fear of jail or by the fact that you could research the options "just one more time" is not a new phenomenon.

---

[11]Although I will not be franchising....

The ossified decision making of the Vatican has led the way for centuries (remember it was only recently that they ratified the sixteenth-century findings of Copernicus) and I suspect it will now take another few hundred years to agree to name Mother Theresa—surely the greatest nonfictional role model of all time—as a saint. Mindful of my own influence with Pope John Paul the Best Seller, I have contemplated forwarding the name of Prince Charles for a similar honor but have decided not to. He is a dear friend and I know he looks very worthy in his kilt, but I fear there are character flaws. How else do you explain the fact that after every occasion that he has been to our house for luncheon, I have this urge to count the forks?

# 9

## On New Branding
## (and Jolting Your Customer)

The three-toed sloth has much to teach us in business. It's been a while since I've been in the higher reaches of an Amazonian tree watching one, but I am reliably informed that one of its more entertaining habits is to grasp one of its own limbs and mistake it for a tree branch. What happens next is that it obeys the law of gravity, crashes through the foliage, and hits the deck (or "exhibits deck-hitting behavior," as zoologists would say). If you are lucky enough to have a good vantage point you can witness it all: a yelp, a crashing of vegetation, a thud, and a sloth lying there dazed but still clinging on, wondering what went wrong.

Its puzzlement is reasonable. After all it did what sloths are meant to do: took a firm hold and maintained its grip. All should be well, but all is not well. Now I'd like you to think about IBM in the late 1980s and Robert Allen's AT&T in the mid 1990s. Anything appear familiar?[1]

---

[1] "Am I clinging on to my own leg?" is a great self-test to apply in business. Planet Hollywood might not like the answer if they asked the question. Boeing surely wouldn't.

The American Customer Satisfaction Index (ACSI) is a good place to spot next-generation corporate sloths. My personal béte noir is American Airlines (with whom I have two million frequent flyer miles) and I note that their robust policy of jacking up fares for business travelers and then packing them into crowded planes dropped their score a whopping 12.5 percent during 1997 and landed them in 187th place, which is one below the police. This isn't just about price and product; much of it is attitudinal. Along with the delays (my record with them during the last twelve months was a four-hour delay for a fifty-minute flight, a delay during which we were not allowed off the aircraft) and price (I've just paid $1,900 for a coach class ticket from Miami to San Francisco and return; the only direct flight available to me, and don't they just know that), their "hostile monopoly" spirit seems to permeate everybody who puts on their uniform. Recently I had to change a ticket and went personally to American's office in Miami. There were no other customers in the place and there were three service agents standing behind computer terminals at the counter. None of them made eye contact, so I hovered about ten feet away from the counter, wondering which one would crack first. Eventually one looked up and told me (true story) to take a number from the deli-style number roll. I pointed out I was the only one in the place, to which the woman responded that "Somebody might come in" and gave me a look that would have stopped a charging rhino at a hundred yards. I had two choices: spring a leak and yell and scream (and not get my ticket changed) or shut the hell up (and get my ticket and get out of there). I chose the latter.[2]

Further down the ACSI, in a dismal 189th place (only one above the worst surveyed: the IRS) was a slumping (U.S.) McDonald's. I took particular delight in noting that Burger King had now overtaken them (to 171st—not a position to be proud

---

[2]Although the story gets worse, and I couldn't totally hold my "peace and tranquility" strategy. About five minutes later, one of the assistants looked up from her computer, glanced at the screen that showed the next number for service and called, "Number 67, please." At that juncture, I lept from my seat into the air, looked around several times, and then shouted just as loudly, "That must be me." It did not go down well.

of in isolation, but a miracle from where the two brands had been less than a decade ago). The dormant Burger King of the late eighties had three structural customer service problems in the U.S. compared to McDonald's: a crappy service reputation, a family-unfriendly market position, and a high cost structure that was passed on to the consumer in high prices.

It took a huge effort to attack the service issues at Burger King, perhaps the key differentiator with McD's. We put a 1-800 number on every piece of packaging (and then staffed customer service phones twenty-four hours a day); we separated operational audit from line management (who had previously done their own quality audits—a classic case of the fox guarding the chickens); and we instigated a program in which every Burger King was visited once a month by a mystery shopper[3] to report on service standards. We developed a system so that when any of this information came in, it was processed and fed out to line management quickly so they could act where necessary. All the information was synthesized into a Brand Delivery Index, and management bonuses weren't paid if the index fell short of target. In three years we profoundly increased not only the level of service but the awareness of its importance to our brand's success.

Both of the burger giants in the U.S. have transitioned from what I call the old branding to the new branding over the last several years, and their journeys (and successes and failures) are illustrative of what all companies have had to face as the science of branding has changed dramatically over that period.

So what's "new branding"? What are the big differences? My observation is that five structural changes have occurred that are forcing people responsible for brands to reinvent everything associated with the way they think about and manage those brands. Branding today is not just about packets of soap powder; it applies to Big Six accounting, churches, credit cards, sports franchises, and just about every product and service we use.

---

[3]I will now make an appalling admission: I never met a mystery shopper. In some ways, that explains their success—they really were mysterious. All I know is that, if I had been a Burger King restaurant manager, I would have kept my eyes open for any customer weighing more than 300 pounds and made sure they got great service.

On New Branding (and Jolting Your Customer)

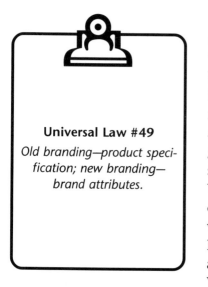

First change: Old branding was about a product or service specification. "Our beer is better than theirs because..." or, "Here is our new, improved toothpaste." Now branding is more about brand attributes that seek fit and comfort with the values of the target market and thus increase the propensity to purchase. Richard Branson, Virgin's rainmaker (who claims, incidentally, that Virgin is Britain's first new worldwide brand in fifty years), defines his brand's attributes as fun, innovative, and offering great value, which enables Virgin to offer a portfolio of products and services ranging from airlines to soft drinks, from financial services to music products. It is this change more than any other that has caused the renaissance of Burger King at the expense of McDonald's in the U.S.: McD's held the high ground in the eighties with the attributes of price value, family friendliness, consistency, and service. Once Burger King hauled itself up to be level (or thereabouts) on these attributes, it was bound to make gains because it has one additional attribute that McD's doesn't have: The food is better.[4]

Branding has also moved from supply-side management thinking to a demand-led approach. Previously the product was the center of the universe and it was mass-marketed to zillions of people on a take-it-or-leave-it basis. Then a Copernicus-like transformation came about: The consumer became the center of the universe and the product

---

[4]I was the happiest CEO in the U.S. when McD's introduced the McLean. My ingoing position on the subject (which has remained intact) is that seaweed and hamburgers each need their own space. A long way away from each other.

was no longer the single entity that mattered. The single entity that matters now is the individual, who will determine to buy according to what he or she determines are important values, not what somebody else intimates should be important. We are entering into an era of mass customization as against mass marketing, an era in which winning companies will know as much about their customers as they would if they were dating agencies. The possibilities were brought home to me when, for a recent birthday present, a friend bought me some golf balls. Now, golf balls have always been marketed in the same way, right? "Here's our tube (packet, whatever) of balls, and they cost this much, but they will go longer or higher or with more accuracy or whatever. Choose ours for these reasons blahblahblah-blah." Contrast that with my birthday present: Through the mail came an egg carton (!) with six golf balls in it. On the front of the carton was my name, and each ball was emblazoned with the badge of St. Andrews (the Scottish ancestral home of golf) and my name. This is probably very small fry today, but the gift came via the Internet and ten years from now, when cyberspace is part of everybody's everyday life, can you imagine what the implications are for branding golf balls and a million other products and services?

Another determining factor in forcing the change from old to new branding has been the improvement in buying standards. After forty years of postwar prosperity, underpinned by corporate and personal comfort and security, both consumer and business buying had become sloppy. When the recession hit at the end of the 1980s, many corporations reengineered their businesses, and one of the first places they looked was procurement. All of a sudden we had companies buying like Wal-Mart: professionally, aggressively, and without compromise. At Burger King we dramatically reshaped the way we bought product (including moving from seventeen suppliers of french fries to one) and the results at the restaurant profitability level were such that we were able to reinvest in the consumers with the Value Meal strategy.

Private consumers also became more savvy buyers. After decades of being underpinned by the security of a job and positive equity in most homes, many families faced the nineties with neither of these. Result? Consumer purchasing became more of a science, with individuals much less likely to take anybody else's word for what held value or didn't. They would make their own minds up, thank you very much.

On an infamous day in 1992 Marlboro, a bastion of the old branding, cut the price of its cigarettes because it was losing share to generic brands, and all hell broke loose. It's as good a day in history as any to signal the advent of new branding, with Wall Street having the opposite of an orgasm,[5] but although the big branding companies (e.g., Coca-Cola) took a short-term hit, branding didn't die. Buyers still wanted distinction and price did not become the only differentiator. But the new generation of buyers wanted real value, and they wanted it by their definition, not by some advertising agency's terms.

New branding, finally, represents a move away from customer satisfaction as a success criteria to the establishment of a customer relationship. Sales figures were replaced by repeat sales figures on many corporate altars as objects of worship, as study after study drove home the two messages: Satisfied customers are still likely to defect, and customer loyalty makes a bundle of economic sense.

How often it was pounded into business school students of the seventies and eighties: Customer satisfaction is *key*, so make sure you measure it and take action on the results. That might have been fine for the world of old branding, but in the brave new world there is clear evidence that satisfaction is not enough. A Bain and Co. study (*Fortune* magazine, September

---

[5]I'm not sure what this is called, but I know one when I see it.

1994) highlights the inadequacy of tracing satisfaction as a success criteria, noting that 60 to 80 percent of customers who end up defecting typically describe themselves as satisfied or very satisfied. Thomas Jones and Earl Sasser, who authored (what for me is) the definitive work on the subject in the *Harvard Business Review* (November 1995), drove home the point in terms even the most mouth-breathing of mass marketers can understand. Scoring satisfaction on a scale of 1 to 5, with 3 and 4 representing satisfied and very satisfied, only those customers recording a 5 (definition: *completely* satisfied) showed loyalty. The 3s and 4s were "easily switched to a competitor." With one stroke, these guys defined the success criteria for new branding: complete satisfaction—no compromise.

**Universal Law #52**

*Old branding—customer satisfaction; new branding—customer relationships.*

There is a follow-up dimension to this thinking that makes it even more important for new branding. The loyalty that can be achieved by pursuing the Holy Grail of complete satisfaction can be hugely profitable. Many companies, if they took the trouble to find out, would find that a kind of "satisfaction-pareto" principle is at work in their businesses, that the bulk of their profitability (that's profit, not sales) comes from a minority of their customer base—their "regulars." They tend to buy more, buy more often, and need less attention (read *cost*) than the market floaters, yet very few companies pay enough attention to the customers they have, chasing the business equivalent of a one-night stand instead. The possible payback from doing this differently? The Bain study estimates that a decrease in customer defections of 5 percent can boost profits by 25 to 90 percent.

New branding must attempt this new success criterion with the same old materials, so essentially it becomes how you mix the cocktail of price, product (or service) specification, and the relationship with the buyer. They're the same old ingredients that the old brand mangers had, but the old mix won't do anymore. We also begin to see why the third of the three ingredients—the relationship with the customer—is so important in the new branding mix. In simple terms, it is the easiest one to adapt to the four imperatives we defined earlier for new branding. Sure, there are companies who thrive in the new world with product excellence heavy in their cocktail mix (Gillette) or with price a dominant factor (Price CostCo, Dell Computers), but the vast majority has found that enhancing the (service) relationship with the customer has been the key.

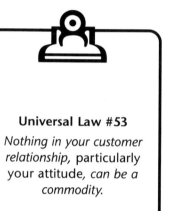

**Universal Law #53**

*Nothing in your customer relationship,* **particularly your attitude,** *can be a commodity.*

So let's invent some universal laws together, the first one being that nothing (*nothing*) you do in the relationship with the customer can be a commodity. In case you missed it the first time: **n-o-t-h-i-n-g**. A lot of folks think I am rambling on about product specification here, but that's the last place I start. This is about an attitude of mind. It's a mind-set that insists every aspect of your relationship with the customer is memorable, zany, bizarre, exhilarating, wacky, or all of the above. It's a frame of mind that has some flight attendants on Southwest Airlines taking the most boring (commodity) act in commercial life (the safety speech at the beginning of a flight) and *singing it.*[6] It's where, as Tom Peters put it (in the long-running 1997 debate in *Fast Company* magazine), the brand becomes *you*. It's where I go ballistic when Big Six accountants come up to me and say, "What can we do? All we do is get customers' audit results on time." My response? Tell 'em if they're not on time the whole audit team will turn up one Saturday morning

---

[6] Since this occurrence I've been listening to it, and I'm not happy. What's with these life jackets that you might have to "top up" by blowing into those two little pipes? If you've ditched in the Atlantic, with Europe 2500 miles one way and the U.S. 1500 back t'other way, I don't want "top-up" crap. I want *no leaking* as a base specification. Some telescopic oars and a wee outboard motor would also come in handy.

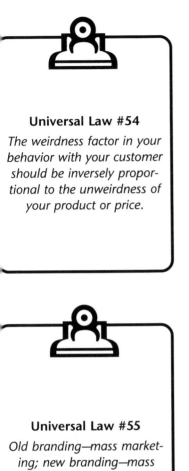

**Universal Law #54**

*The weirdness factor in your behavior with your customer should be inversely proportional to the unweirdness of your product or price.*

**Universal Law #55**

*Old branding—mass marketing; new branding—mass customization.*

and wash all the clients' cars. Do weird stuff, the weirder the better. The weirdness factor in your behavior in relationship with the customer needs to be inversely proportional to the unweirdness of your product specification or price.

Second universal law: Abandon mass marketing; think mass customization. The Internet has only just started to reveal the possibilities where this science is involved, but there is plenty of scope with the tools available today. Mass customization is not just about product specification (although you should remember my golf balls). It can be about big brands thinking small or local. It can also be about marketing to a tight group of individuals. For example, much of Cadillac's effort is focused on the televised Senior Golf Tour. They know exactly who is watching.

We go upstream a bit for the next law: Loyal customers are more likely to stay that way if you have loyal and empowered employees dealing with them. A couple of brave companies are recognizing this as *the* key to the door of new branding, and I love Hal Rosenbluth's work on the subject. He's the CEO of Rosenbluth International (a Philadelphia-based travel management company) and his approach is quite clear from the title of his book, *The Customer Comes Second and Other Secrets of Exceptional Service.*[7] Another wacky idiot? Last time I looked, his company had a client reten-

---

[7]Hal Rosenbluth, *The Customer Comes Second and Other Secrets of Exceptional Service* (Quill, 1994).

**Universal Law #56**

*Guess what? Loyal customers like dealing with the same people.*

**Universal Law #57**

*Regularly jolt (or startle) your customer into recognizing (or remembering) how good you are. A sloth's orgasm is (roughly) the impact you should seek.*

tion rate of 90 percent and its employee turnover rate was 6 percent—mind-blowing for that industry. Subliminal message: Next time you're considering downsizing, cost into it some potential lost customer loyalty. If you think about it for more than ten minutes, you might start to get scared.

The last law is all my own and I call it the jolt factor law. Even if you are getting all of the above right, it still might not be enough to create the level of enthusiasm or excitement (or whatever) in the relationship from the customer's vantage point to create genuine loyalty. Now and again you need to do something that startles them—jolts them—into recognizing just how good you are and what attributes (remember?) you stand for. George Zimmer, CEO of Men's Warehouse, insists his salespeople call every customer 15 days after they buy a suit to make sure everything is okay. Now, that call would wake me up for the day. Recently I was enjoying a dinner in a restaurant that I hadn't visited before. Service was a bit sluggish, but no big deal. Suddenly the manager appeared at the side of our table and told us that he was unhappy about the way his kitchen was performing that night, and that there would be no charge for the meal. Wow! What planet did *he* come from?[8] (P.S. I'm now a regular customer). Ritz Carlton employees can spend $2,000 to redress a guest's grievance; can you imagine the jolt that could deliver? The loyalty it would generate? New branding folks have realized that this is cheap marketing.

---

[8]And just how long would *he* last in an American Airlines front office?

I'm going back to my pal the sloth to find what we're looking for here—a definition of the jolt factor. Please don't ask me the source or how it came into my possession, but I once possessed a copy of a graph tracing (Are you ready?) the pulse rate of the three-toed sloth during the act of mating. It was truly a magnificent sight (the graph, that is). The line trundled along the bottom (time) axis for what seemed like hours, then suddenly, reflecting what can only be called a sloth orgasm, it took off like a rocket, shooting up through three sheets of graph paper for about a twelve-second span. Then it slumped down to the baseline again and carried on there, presumably while our hero fumbled for a cigarette or a book to read.

Picture that graph in your mind. Remember it. *That* is a jolt. New branding demands that you apply one of those immediately to any of your loyal customers who have a complaint, and every few weeks to those who haven't. Nothing less will work.

# 10

## On Innovation

For some reason I've grown to love things Italian. One of my favorite watering holes in Florida is a small trattoria that provides everyday Italian food of profound integrity. This is weird because its owners are Argentinian and Dutch.

I was in there recently, languidly contemplating an osso bucco with an estimated street value of $1.2 million[1] when I started, for some reason, thinking about innovators. At first this must seem a quantum leap for most of you because, apart from Garibaldi (who invented a biscuit), the famous Second World War tank they developed (which retreated faster than it went forward), and Mussolini (who invented four million soldiers by assuming he had five million in his army when he declared war in 1941), the Italians are not noted for a history of innovation.[2]

Well, they may not have had a long string of innovators, but what the Italians lost in quantity they made up for in quality. Here I confess my attraction to a certain group of these breakthrough folks who have left their mark indelibly on the

[1]This is Miami, remember.

[2]Just as Belgium is noted for never having produced anybody famous.

history books: the daft ones. In that category, without hesitation, I give you the emperor Nero, who many believe is famous only for fiddling while Rome burned,[3] but whose real claim to fame makes that pale by comparison. He was the first guy to purify water by boiling it, an act, I'm sure you'll agree, of somebody blessed with an innovative, analytical mind. If he were alive today, he would already be working on Windows 2111. However—and this is what endears him (and his particular breed) to me—he promptly negated the beneficial breakthrough nature of his idea by cooling the resultant pure water with infected ice he had specially brought down from the mountains every day.

He would not be a loner today. Innovation is driving an unprecedented pace of change in every aspect of life—the ways we eat and drink, communicate, doctor ourselves, transport ourselves, entertain ourselves, and work. We are not even constrained to Earth anymore. We get oil from under the sea. We can source fresh food from anywhere and deliver it to anywhere, any time. We can digitally mix film and video footage so that Fred Astaire can dance with a new carpet cleaning device in a TV ad. There seems to be no limit to the ways in which civilization can benefit from innovation.

Innovation is the key to effective new branding (I am openly checking whether you read the last chapter or are just browsing in the bookstore[4]). It can have a material effect on all three variables we covered, one of them in a rather surprising way.

For most people, it would appear that the actual product (or service) specification would be the most fertile area for innovation to support the search for complete customer satisfaction, and there are companies (Gillette and Sony, for exam-

---

[3]He didn't. He couldn't have. In the spirit of the extensive technical research that is the hallmark of this book, I am here to tell you the fiddle had not been invented when Nero strode the stage of the known world. The lyre had been invented, so he might have lyred while Rome burned....

[4]If you are in the bookstore and contemplating buying this book, you should know that one copy is rarely enough for the properly equipped modern home. It is de rigueur to have one in each bathroom, with several others positioned strategically around the house and at the office. The genuinely upwardly mobile will make exciting gifts of this book after dinner parties.

ple) that blaze this trail. Others believe that innovative pricing is key to developing a winning formula, and that also can be achieved. Tesco drew well ahead in the fierce U.K. supermarket wars in the mid 1990s with a creative loyalty scheme, which is just a fancy form of discounting your prices. In Burger King in the U.S. innovative pricing helped the brand totally reposition itself in the first half of the nineties. Apart from the Kid's Club meals (a combination of a discounted meal and a premium toy put together in special packaging), the Value Meal concept did much to support the family-friendly repositioning. It is often taken to an even more (!) innovative level: You will frequently see a big external sign for a "99-Cent Whopper" outside a Burger King, but when you go inside, there's no sign of it. The individual value Whopper is bundled up and sold as part of the Value Meal with high-margin fries and a drink.

Innovations in pricing and product specification are the obvious ones, but the least obvious one should not be forgotten. Innovation in your relationship with your customer gets to the core of what I believe to be the huge opportunity of new branding: the constant challenge to reinvent your own approach to how you do things. It's about how you think as well as how you behave. It needs what Allen Sheppard of GrandMet once described to me as a "permanent state of restlessness." It's a mentality that questions every day: "If I landed from another planet today, how would I go about doing what I do?" The answer might be so different from the status quo it's scary—the answer might even be that *you wouldn't even do it*. Neither answer scares the true innovators. The only thing that scares them is maintaining the status quo.

**Universal Law #58**

*In business, a permanent state of restlessness is a wonderful disease to have.*

Veteran rock stars (the "geyser rockers") have a lot to teach the corporate world, and some of them handle this aspect brilliantly. McCartney saw the Beatles as a means, not an end (contrast that thinking with Ringo); he saw his work in the sixties as his heritage, on which he could build a brand new entity. In 1997 he topped the classical music charts as well as having a hit with a conventional rock album, and he fills stadiums today just as well as he ever did—thirty years at the top of one of the most competitive markets in the world. Clapton changes his hairstyle, clothes, eyeglasses, and music genre every two years (like clockwork), but still offers the world the same core competency and brand name. Paul Simon constantly seeks new challenges. Many will scoff at his failure on Broadway, citing that as evidence to support conservatism and a stick-with-the-program philosophy. Baloney. Simon will be back bigger and better for having has a single failure. All we have witnessed is that it is not in his makeup to do a Don McLean and sing "American Pie" every night for thirty years.

The need to innovate mentally is one missed in most essays on the subject. In the world of new branding, however, it can turn a ho-hum product, delivered at a ho-hum price, into a market beater.

The level of innovation today, in all its forms, is scary. It needs to be because if it wasn't, Malthus would by now have been deemed one of history's optimists. Despite the ascent of man and woman, our Earth and its population seem to have an astonishing ability to throw up wars, pestilence, and disasters to a level that we've needed a crazy pace of innovation over the last couple of centuries just to hang in there.

Innovation is also having a profound effect on the wealth of nations. Recorded inflation, which does more to damage wealth than most other things, is running at low single-digit growth rates in many developed countries, and relatively low in most others. In reality, a strong case can be made that even these figures overstate real inflation if you factor in the (innovative) quality improvements in goods and services that are bought for the marginal year-by-year price increases. On a like-for-like basis, the cost of many goods and services is declining.

All that's fine, but the amount of money that's now going into research and new product development is frightening. In business, every company feels the need to innovate at unprecedented levels—from small, undercapitalized start-ups, through the mid-size organizations fighting to sustain organic growth, right through to the giants who are trying to stay that way. It is rumored that the aggregate U.S. investments in these activities in pharmaceuticals, weaponry, telecommunications, transportation, and data processing alone now equal the gross receipts of a single Jimmy Buffet concert.

All that investment money—whether it is sourced by revenues, equity, or debt—needs to make a return or be serviced. I put that scary fact up there alongside the knowledge that there are about sixteen trillion dollars invested in the derivative markets, just to help you all sleep at night. If only we knew how to account for the latter.

At the turn of this century the German chemist, Von Bayer, was working in the U.S. in a laboratory in the basement of his house. He needed an innovative breakthrough, ironically in physics, that would enable him to mix chemicals consistently over long periods of time. His team of chemists worked on the problem and triumphed and, unable to contain his excitement,[5] Von Bayer called his wife downstairs to share his moment of glory. She took one look at it and happily informed him that what they had produced would be ideal for her making of mayonnaise.[6] Today that system still forms the basis for mass mayonnaise production.

I now call this the Mayonnaise Factor (MF), and it is the key to the whole innovation challenge. It is crucial to figure out what is really needed by your end user, and then supply that and nothing else. There is a

**Universal Law #59**
*Figure out what your user will really need, and innovate to that end. Do not innovate just because you can.*

---

[5]My observation is that Von Bayer needed to get a life.

[6]Look, I have nothing against wives. I am married to a wonderful one. But why, oh why do they do this? Why can they not seem to share moments of demented male joy? On the rare occasions my soccer team puts the ball in the correct goal (i.e., the opposition's), I leap about in my seat and make Jim Carrey look like a resigning Japanese finance minister. My wife's contribution to the proceedings is to try very hard to humor me with a supportive smile.

huge propensity today to innovate just because you can. The boundaries of many of our sciences suddenly look very close and flimsy because of the geometric growth in our ability to process and analyze information—and to experiment with and produce new products and processes. For big corporations, the demand to innovate seems like the demand on health care: almost infinite. The temptation to try to cover every base must be huge, but for businesses of all sizes the rewards for winning are enormous and the cost of losing is potentially ruinous. The key is spotting the MF.

Nowhere is the challenge more profound than in the increasingly overlapping worlds of computing and telecommunications. Andy Groves, who is noted for dealing with his prostate cancer with the same sort of quiet reserve you would normally associate with, say, a Three Tenors concert, is head of the quite extraordinary Intel Corporation. He recently reeled off some of his own forecasts for chip technology developments over the next decade or so. Today's Pentium Pro microprocessor chip contains 5.5 million transistors, and by the year 2011 it will pack about a billion. Today's top clock speed of 200 megahertz will soar to 10 gigahertz (10,000 megahertz) by then. I would be enormously impressed by this if it weren't for the feeling that I only use about fifteen of my current transistors and wouldn't recognize a Pentium chip if it bit me in the groin. As Bobby Jones, the veteran golfer, once commented when confronted by a young Jack Nicklaus: "He plays a game of golf with which I am not familiar."

I am a keen user of Intel's products, possessing both a desktop PC and a laptop. My own guesstimate[7] is that I am within the one percent of the world's population that accesses a computer daily. But there is a huge difference between my MF and that of the really serious users, who are probably one percent of the one percent that I'm in. I have never adopted the Lewis Grizzard approach ("I will never type anything on anything that doesn't have a moving ribbon.") and I use my word

[7]This follows an extensive focus group and research program on this subject undertaken in John Martin's Irish bar in Coral Gables, Miami. The results were all written down on a beer mat, but I've lost it.

processor, spreadsheets, and organizer daily. I am also an enthusiastic user of the Web and E-mail and never cease to marvel at how technology has changed the way I do so many things. Yet it's difficult to fit me in the picture with Intel, who is spending $2 billion on new factories before the need for them has been formally identified so that I can have a billion transistors on my chip thirteen years from now. Andy, stop and smell the roses a while. Thirteen years from now I still won't be using the transistors I've got now. However, if you could turn your innovative genius to addressing the challenge of my not being treated like dog doo every time I use an airport and a plane, you would have my vote as innovator of the century.

I suppose, nonetheless, I am an attractive future market target in this area, so let's use me as a test. Just what is my MF? Is the epicenter of my needs going to polarize to my PC or to my TV? Already technology exists to put a (sort of) boom box into the back of my TV on which I can play CDs, see my family photographs on another sort of CD, and get interactive with another kind of CD. I'll shortly have DVD (digital video disc) on which I can stockpile my favorite movies and concerts instead of having to use those pesky tapes that need rewinding. I'll probably access the Web through my TV...or...will I do virtually all this through my PC?...or both?...or something else? Today, millions of dollars are backing potential innovations covering every possible combination, without any real evidence as to where my real MF will lie. If anybody our there figures it out, you are on to a lottery win—and I'd also be grateful if you'd let me know. I have no idea.

Getting innovation right—in your product, your pricing, or your mental and behavioral modus operandi—means hiring the right people. Nor more people in lab coats or more nerds. Nor does everybody in the business need replacing. You need enough restless, innovative minds in your company mix to do the technical jobs *and* rub off on everybody else so that they, in turn, catch the innovation disease.

I've always been fascinated by what happened when man first got milk from a cow. I mean the very, *very*, **very** first time.

Just what was the guy thinking? What kind of mind says to itself: "I'm going over there to that beast, and I'm gonna pull on that thing (or those things[8]), and drink what comes out"? Trust me, this is not the kind of mind that you want next to you on a trans-Atlantic flight. Yet this is the kind of mind that changed the world's diet.

**Universal Law #60**

*To develop an innovative culture, you need to hire some Jack Nicholsons in your team's mix. (That's Jack in* The Shining.) *It's not always comfortable, but you need some weird minds in there with you—minds that, if they were soup, you'd eat with a long* spoon.

There's the conundrum. Innovators sometimes appear like Jack Nicholson—that's Jack in *The Shining*, not Jack in *As Good As It Gets*—but they're the ones who deliver the winning ideas for you. Somehow you have to encompass a few mavericks in your corporate team, which is not always easy since (sometimes) corporate teams can be a wee bit conservative and sometimes these folks don't fit in easily. They can bring you unpleasant news, like telling you, after you've just started to gain market share, that your product already needs a radical overhaul. They don't tell you to do something cheaper, faster, or better—they tell you to do something *else*. They tell lifelong retailers that the way to reach the consumer in the future will be without an outlet. They were the ones who told Toyota that it shouldn't call its up-market cars by that name; how 'bout Lexus? They are restless and ornery. They think the unthinkable. They're the ones who search for completely unexplainable success when the rest are compiling sophisticated reasons for failing. When everybody has figured out the finite six options available to the business, they come up with a seventh.

It is wrong to stereotype innovators as mad professors or nerds. They come in all shapes and sizes and are not gender-restricted. They do have one thing in common: They are never comfortable, nor do they let anybody else become so. They are

---

[8]Well, he didn't know at that stage, did he? During the research phase he may well have tried to milk a bull. The results of this experiment are not known.

often a pain in the butt to work with, but when you find one, treasure him or her.

Every aspect of your search for market distinction can be supported by innovation. As the word implies, it is not about chips or technology—it is about being new. Nordstrom's innovative approach to service provides real distinction, but has its basis in new attitudes and behavior.

Of course, occasionally innovators get it wrong, and the results often indicate the fine line between glorious success and the corporate equivalent of "most embarrassing moments." Most of you would cite New Coke as an innovation from hell, or possibly Sony's first launch of the mini-disc, but I have a much better one. Oh, my word, yes.

**Universal Law #61**

*Innovation is not just about chips and technology—it is about being new. New attitudes and behavior can be just as effective in the marketplace.*

I give you Geoffrey Nathaniel Pyke (1894–1948), innovator extraordinaire. This guy was on Mountbatten's central staff in England during the Second World War, and was forever coming up with ideas to speed up our victory. His best—and certainly most ambitious—was code-named *Habbakuk* and involved (Are you ready?) a battleship made of ice. This was to have been a huge boat, several times the size of the world's (then) biggest liner, the *Queen Mary*. It would be unsinkable, and a torpedo would only make a slight dent in its hull that could be quickly repaired. He had worked out how to keep it frozen, how it would be powered and steered, and, best of all, how it would fight. Shrugging off bombs and torpedoes, it would sail into enemy ports and capture enemy ships by spraying them with super-cooled water, encasing them in ice, and forcing them to surrender. But his plan didn't stop there—oh, no. Special teams would then infiltrate the countryside, spraying railway tunnels and freezing trains and so on...presumably until we captured a Hitler popsicle.

What fascinates me is not the wildness of the plan, but the enthusiasm shown for it by the normally sanguine group of Mountbatten, Churchill, Roosevelt, and the Allied Chiefs of Staff when they met at Quebec during the war. *Habbakuk* was given the green light and was only aborted because the Normandy landings changed the nature of the challenge. Sadly, the project never saw the light of day, and that is a great tragedy for the moviemaker James Cameron, if for nobody else. *Habbakuk* would have made *Titanic* look like light comedy.

It would never have worked, you see. I am sorry to end this session on effective innovation on such a negative note, but I have spotted a mortal failing in the great ice-battleship project, a flaw that none of the other great minds worked out for themselves. It concerns noise. I believe it would have been impossible to concentrate on making war accompanied by the din of the frozen testicles of the male members of the crew dropping with a resounding *thunk* onto the (presumably) steel decking. Just impossible.

# 11

## On Surviving
## in the New Job

It's a wee bit long ago for my own comfort, but at the height[1] of my amateur soccer career I remember our team going through the trauma of having a new coach come in and take over. The appointment itself surprised us all, because he was one of the regular guys in the league that we played against week in and week out—he was really one of "us," not "them." There is a particular peer group chemistry among English amateur soccer players that comes from sharing a very cold winter locker room while you are all naked,[2] and the idea of this guy suddenly being our manager made for a lot of quiet moments as we approached our first match.

Saturday arrived and we started going through the pre-match rituals, rubbing ourselves all over with an excruciating mixture of horse linament and deep heat ointment,[3] when suddenly the door opened and in he came. The moment had arrived

---

[1]The word *height* does not bear up to any deep analysis based on the Harvard qualifier, i.e., compared to what?

[2]There is nowhere to hide.

[3]I'm giving away trade secrets here, but it was an important part of our collective team psyche that even if we weren't fit, we smelled fit.

for the (and his) first great leadership speech. Standing on a bench, he coughed, paused dramatically, then uttered the immortal words: "I've been outside lads, and there's a wind blowing down the pitch. If we win the toss, play against it in the first half. But remember, if you do, to kick your high balls low." He then swept—that's the only word that describes it—out of the room, where we remained in complete silence for about twenty seconds before imploding with mirth. I remember thinking, as I ran out onto the pitch, that this was the first time I had genuinely cried since I was about seven years old.

I wish, I *wish* I had noted some of his ensuing pre-match speeches; they were true jewels. I do remember playing the first part of one game in pain after being motivated by the idea that "It's not natural to be natural, lads." To this day I have no idea what he meant, but I also remember throwing it down the boardroom table in Burger King once (when I was having a bad hair day) and a lot of folks nodded thoughtfully. At least one wrote it down.

Ever since that famous day in our humble locker room I have been fascinated by the chemistry surrounding new appointments, particularly in business, and by what makes us pick the people we pick and why it goes wrong so often. The mortality rate for new appointees in business—and indeed the infant mortality rate, meaning failure in the first few weeks—is one of the embarrassing elements of modern business, particularly when you consider the levels of both art and science that go into the selection procedures for key positions today.

The reasons why new appointments go wrong are easy to define in principle: The employee can behave suboptimally, the employer can do the same, and the process that should monitor and appraise the situation can fail. It only needs one of these to occur and the good ship *New Appointment* is foundering, but what is astonishing is how often *all three* happen simultaneously. When this occurs, the ship is holed below the water line.

There are three ways newly appointed employees themselves can contribute to failure, and in the first one it's kinda hard to figure out who is really to blame. The reality is that, however thoroughly the employer researches the employee and vice versa, you cannot tell how it's actually going to work until he or she sits in the chair and does the job. Sure, both sides can do a whole lot of stuff to minimize the risk, but until you're in real-time you will not know for sure, and stuff can pop out of the woodwork at that stage that will amaze everybody concerned.

When I left Burger King I had completed two years as CEO and three more as Chairman and CEO. This was after a decade of leadership turbulence in which (I think) seven leaders had come and gone, and we wanted the changeover from me to my successor to be as seamless as possible. We decided to recruit my successor a full year before I left and work with him to make sure there were no surprises and few risks when the eventual coronation occurred. Now, bear in mind one of the things I think I did well as a manager was to recognize early on that the key to success was to pick the right people and have them succeed, and on the back of that I had established a reputation as a really good judge of corporate horse flesh. So you would think that given the luxury of (effectively) a 365-day interview, I would make a good choice. The truth is I bollixed it up and made the biggest judgment error of my career. Five days after the appointment I knew I'd got it wrong, and that fact played a part in my deciding that my thirty-year marriage to big business was coming to an end.

Don't get me wrong: Measured by the normal corporate criteria the guy was successful at Burger King, and probably successful by all his own criteria. He has since moved elsewhere and is successful by the same measures, and probably will continue to be so. What tripped me up was that I made the judgment on additional criteria of my own, convinced myself there was a bucketload of evidence of some particular qualities I wanted, and was then genuinely surprised when I found I'd appointed a stranger. We can now note the first universal law: However long you have to research an appointee,

**Universal Law #62**
*However long you have to interview a candidate, you will find out something new about him or her within five days after the person actually starts the job.* Watch out for *it, and be prepared to respond.*

you will find out something new about him or her within five days after the person actually starts the job. *Watch out for it*, and be prepared to respond.

Another way the employee can sabotage a new appointment is by trying to force an unnatural change in his or her own behavior in response to some perceived need that the new situation demands it. This is particularly popular when a promotion is involved, and even more so when the promotion is from a peer group. The reality is there usually are different talents required, often involving fewer task skills and more people and process abilities in the mix (none more so than in my beloved soccer coach, who moved from playing soccer to selecting, preparing, and motivating a team to play). Far too often, however, people respond to this challenge by abandoning some of the very strengths that got them promoted in the first place. Overnight, sensitive human beings become complete SOBs, common-sense communicators start to talk in meaningless maxims, easygoing psyches turn paranoid, and balanced personalities become monomaniacs. The even worse news is that some of these traits are taken home.

**Universal Law #63**

*If you have been offered a new job, pause to figure out which of your strengths have been identified in relation to the challenge ahead. Then be sensible enough not to abandon them.*

The irony is that modern management requires more of the skills that most people feel they must discard when they finally reach the executive floor. It is likely that a winning salesperson will not be appointed as sales manager based on his or her ability to sell a lot of widgets, but because someone has seen in him or her hidden abilities that are needed to manage salespeople. It would be a great help in making appointments successful if appointees would pause to figure out just why they are being appointed and what their real strengths are in relation to what lies ahead, not behind, and then to promise themselves to be brave enough not to abandon those strengths.

I need to be careful in describing the third way the employee can contribute to the failure of a new appointment because it may be more of a male thing, and I'm delighted to note that more and more substantive management appointments are being landed by the fairer sex. As all of you know, life for most males of the human species is just a series of king-of-the-mountain contests, and this is never more pertinent than when a man has just been appointed to a new position and feels the world (and possibly some other planets as well) is watching him closely. It is not unusual to flounder in the crucial first fifty days of a new appointment; in fact quite the opposite is true. The learning curve challenge often seems the equivalent of sprinting up one of Everest's more difficult faces. You usually want to change everything but you're not sure why or how; everybody is trying to get you to sign off on a pet project (that your predecessor turned down repeatedly); and your boss is looking for early signs of a business return on the investment in you as a human resource. It is perfectly normal to flounder on occasion in these circumstances, but how you respond to that is an important element in making the appointment a long-term success. Quite simply, most people will say nothing, afraid that saying anything would be a signal of weakness. Some stay silent and hope the weather clears, some try to bluff their way through (a hugely risky strategy if it goes wrong; credibility can be permanently damaged), and others follow the game plan of our youngest son—when he gets in a hole, he digs.

Several times during my first few weeks at Burger King I was temporarily unclear about which end was up. I had no qualms; I asked for help from above, alongside, or below. The universal rule: It is not *if* you flounder early in a new appointment, it is *when.* Recognize it when it happens, swallow your pride, *and ask for help.*

**Universal Law #64**

*It is not if you flounder early in a new appointment, but when. Recognize it when it happens, swallow your pride, and ask for help.*

Now let's have a look at the creative ways the employer can contribute to the premature death of a new appointment. The debate often centers on the relative merits of making an internal appointment versus going outside, but I think that is of zero relevance. There can be no universal rule on this, as every single appointment reflects a unique set of circumstances. Some companies spend huge amounts of money (Intel, for example, invests a whopping 6 percent of payroll) on training their own management for future challenges, and others have extensive management development systems (Citibank tracks 10,000 employees worldwide) all in an effort to "grow their own" and recruit and replace from within. My observation is that a 100 percent policy either way is nonsense. All things being equal it makes sense for a variety of reasons to recruit from inside—but all things aren't always equal. Sometimes your business needs an injection of outside thinking, and on other occasions it's a sound practice to test your own candidates against the market. It was rare that I would assemble a short list for a key position without at least one outsider on it, and then I didn't give a damn about who got the position, provided it was the best candidate. I was happier if an internal candidate won, but business isn't about being happy.

**Universal Law #65**

*The easy part is to appoint candidates on the basis of their identified strengths. The hard part is remembering their identified weaknesses, and putting in place processes that support and control the appointee in spite of them.*

So, no universal laws on promoting internal versus external candidates, because I don't think that's where the employers get it wrong. Where they fail is in mixing up empowerment with abdication. Empowerment is simply another redundant word (invented by Human Resources) for trust. When a new appointment has been made, often after exhaustive interviews and research by the employer, the tendency is to back off in the interests of something deemed to be empowerment. You've done the hard part, matched the person with the challenge and made the appointment, and now it is important you get out of the way and give the appointee crystal clear accountability and responsibility. What a crock. That is blatant abdication of your responsibility as an employer, and probably the biggest single factor in the widespread demise of new appointments. Most employers, when they consider candidates for a position, analyze both their strengths and weaknesses. What happens is that they make the appointment on the basis of the strengths, then forget the weaknesses, assuming some kind deity will rub vanishing cream on them. The easy part is appointing on the basis of the strengths. The hard part is remembering the weaknesses and putting in place processes that both support and control the candidate in spite of those weaknesses. This is not an erosion of empowerment; it is underpinning success.

Employers are also usually the most culpable when the success of new appointments is threatened by what I call the CIA factor—Confusion from Implied Assumptions. I staggered myself the other day by listing the new appointments I had undertaken in thirty years of life in big corporations (Shell U.K., Whitbread PLC, and GrandMet). The list totaled more than twenty, and as I reflected on each of them in turn, the ambiguities I recalled about what exactly was expected of me in each appointment were astonishing. In most cases I set off with goals that I thought were clearly agreed to, only to find that what assumptions I had inferred from conversations with my appointers and what they really wanted were (in some cases profoundly) different things. Sometimes this is a result of laziness, sometimes something more sinister, but it is dumb for whatever reason. It is imperative for the success of any appointment that both parties agree on a limited number of 100-day goals right from the get-go. What's almost as important is agreeing what's left off that list—things that you both agree can wait or should assume a lower priority.

**Universal Law #66**

*The success of any appointment depends on avoiding the CIA factor (Confusion from Implied Assumptions). Appointor and appointee should agree on a limited number of 100-day goals from the start. They should also agree on what isn't going to get done.*

So we have a situation in which appointer and appointee both invest a huge amount in an appointment and are overtly committed to its success and yet, independently or collectively, often unknowingly and almost always without intent, they sabotage it.

When the third factor then kicks in—the process that should underpin success actually works against it—we begin to see why mortality rates are so high. I refer, of course, to the processes of corporate appraisal and review that should monitor and support performance in all appointments (but that is particularly important for new ones), and I need to digress a little before I attack this subject.

I have mentioned elsewhere that the O. J. Simpson criminal trial verdict left me uncomfortable, a feeling that has not eased with the passing of time. I still wonder which of the two words—*blindingly* or *obvious*—inhibited the jury.

But that's not the real reason for my discomfort. For some years now I have contemplated killing Richard Clayderman. I watched O. J.'s trial, therefore, with deep interest. But it seems to me you have to go through an awful lot of hassle and expense—not to mention more than 400 days in custody—to get a plain ol' "not guilty" verdict for a routine ol' homicide. So I will let him live, but the fact remains that I get barking mad at this European pianist whose music emanates from the speaker systems in every elevator on earth. He just ignites something in me that normally lies dormant.[4] The only other time I have felt like this in recent memory was after my last corporate annual performance appraisal.

This pagan ritual is now institutionalized in most businesses, and it's become so entertaining and hilarious that companies that are sliding below their earnings forecast should bridge the gap by selling tickets. What happens is that once a year, a reluctant manager and an even more reluctant subordinate get together to formally record the latter's performance in the job and maybe to talk about future prospects and develop-

---

[4]Baseball players who chew tobacco also have this effect. For some reason, so does Gene Wilder.

ment plans. Marks are frequently given like they are for ice dancing—although in fairness I have never been involved in one with a Russian judge present.[5]

I find the whole concept rib-tickling. It also is misconceived, badly designed, appallingly executed, and usually does far more damage than good. But it does play an important positive role in business today. There is simply not enough to laugh at in the miserable world of capitalism so this process' critical, and probably only, contribution is its infusion of hilarity into the workplace.

Performance appraisal is getting dafter by the year. For some reason modern management hates anything confrontational, so we've had to change the old practice of sitting down with someone to talk about their strengths and *weaknesses*. Weaknesses? Omygod. We can't suggest that,[6] so now we talk about *areas for development*. Isn't that wonderful? We will shortly reclassify them as *strengthettes*.

Fear and paranoia rule business today, and that causes most appraisals to be stillborn. The following should be the core content of about ten million of them each year:

> **Supervisor:** "Hey, you are not going to grow vertically in this organization, but that's okay. Let's have a reality check here. We're investing in technology, we don't need as many people, those who we do need must have different skills, and we're going to base them in Taiwan. We're just not going to have the structure to provide for regular promotion anymore and in truth, it would not be in the interests of the business or you to give you a bigger job. But I repeat, that's okay.
>
> "But we need you and want you to stay. We need you to broaden your skills and responsibilities, and we will help you do that. We need to complement some of the fast-track people with some stability to give us a well-balanced workforce."
>
> **Supervised:** "Wow. You know, that's really cool. I was really worried that if I got another promotion I would be going beyond my ability and risking real failure—with the atten-

---

[5]Yet. It can only be a matter of time before some mouthbreathing HR official invents the independent judging panel.

[6]That would probably induce a lawsuit.

dant possibility of mental breakdown, divorce, homelessness, incontinence, bankruptcy, and probably several sexual harrassment charges."[7]

That conversation never takes place, of course. Managers are scared because, if the contents reached their supervisors, they might be considered weak to be sticking with employees who are past their shelf life. And the subordinates? If they ever hear a speech like that they know it is all over. Next downsizing, they're going to be history.

So the futility continues: unreal analysis and unreal promises, both of which probably get factored into an unreal management development plan for the whole organization. This freaking circus is turned into neat ratios for "management cover" and "succession planning"—books and books of the stuff that will then be left for dead until they are dusted down for an update next year. The entire exercise reminds me of those Second World War movies, with several serious staff officers moving little ships around on large table maps with a long stick: Everything is neat and official, but there's no real understanding of the capability of any of the ships.

**Universal Law #67**

*You cannot review performance once a year. If you're FUBARing, you need to know this week, not next March.*

Of course it is important for a boss and subordinate to take stock, and particularly during the early period of a new appointment, both to review and to plan. But we need changes in the process.

First thing I'd do is change the title and take *performance* out of it. The idea that you can review that once a year is lunacy; it has to be a dynamic process. Most of the time it is best done weekly, and not written down. If you're FUBARing[8] now, you need to know *this week*, not next March. You can't wait a year for surprises.

[7]The latter applies if this review occurs in the Army or Navy. If it's in the Postal Service you must substitute "murder" for "sexual harrassment."

[8]FUBAR: F---- Up Beyond All Recognition.

I'd focus the whole process on the future, and I'd insist the review itself was done away from the normal place of work. This kind of session needs preplanning, careful thought, concentration, and no distractions. Getting off site doesn't guarantee those things, but staying on site pretty much guarantees you won't get them.

The grandparent (i.e., the boss's boss) must be part of the process, both as an arbiter (if necessary) and as a reality check for the organization. You have no idea how much this simple move makes the boss look at the whole process differently. All of a sudden, if bosses don't do it right, they can look like donkey-wallopers.

The *development charter* (which is what I'd call it) should be proposed by the subordinate, based on self-analysis. It should cover development needs for the present and the next career stage (lateral or vertical). It should also include ideas for discretionary personal development in areas that may only indirectly benefit the organization in the short term. The boss's job is to respond and get into discussion structured around *both* challenging and supporting the proposals. This means arguing and shouting, proposing and counter-proposing, laughing and crying, and regrouping if necessary. The only thing that's not allowed is to deviate from the end result—agreeing on the charter.

Keep Human Resources away from the whole process.[9] If this isn't part of the management task I don't know what is. Human Resources has a role to play in shaping the policies to manage people, but

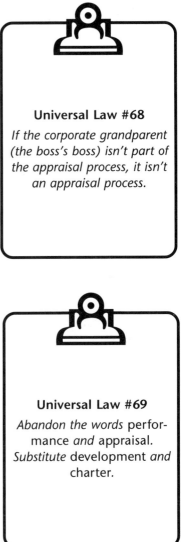

**Universal Law #68**

*If the corporate grandparent (the boss's boss) isn't part of the appraisal process, it isn't an appraisal process.*

**Universal Law #69**

*Abandon the words* performance *and* appraisal. *Substitute* development *and* charter.

---

[9]This will save a ton of money. Reinvest it in developing and training the people.

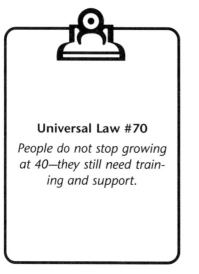

they should keep out of this process. Remember that as you get older you shouldn't suddenly plan to stop growing. The Japanese recognize that you may need more training and support after the age of forty than before, whereas we in the West believe the opposite.[10] We suffer as a result.

It seems that the only thing bigger than the number of forces at work trying to make an appointment a success is the number of counterforces working toward its failure. Yet *everybody* wants the thing to work, and the corroding influences are really just instances of sloppiness and omission. It would seem to take such a little effort to underpin the success of something so important. A friend of mine gave me a wonderful example of how this can work. Upon taking a big CEO-level appointment, he was surprised to see the ousted previous jobholder, who had been forcibly retired, present when he arrived at his new job. Far from being bitter, the veteran gave every bit of help he could to set my friend on his way, and on the day the vet finally left, he handed my friend three numbered envelopes, to open in numeric order if he got in trouble. Sure enough, after a year the business results tanked and my friend opened the first envelope, which held a single piece of paper with the words "Blame your predecessor (me)—I promise you I won't mind" on it. So he did, and the stock market makers bumped his share price back up. A year later trouble returned, so he opened the second envelope and this time was told to"Reengineer." He got his PR department to issue a press release saying that: "To better serve our customers we are laying off 5000 people (etc.)," took a huge charge against earnings, and the stock price promptly recovered again.

---

[10]Why is it the Japanese seem to recognize the obvious so much more clearly than we do?

After another year earnings missed forecast again, so he opened the third envelope. As ever, the advice inside was short and sweet: "Go buy three envelopes."

# 12

# On Information Technology

Way back in the 1960s, I went to see a (then) controversial live musical called *Hair*, which upset a few British vicars because it contained 5.7 seconds of full frontal nudity. I know this because I timed it. It was an eventful evening for me for a couple of reasons. The first was that I took a lifelong vow never to take my pants off on a London theater stage (so far so good). The second was that a particular song ("The Age of Aquarius") caught my imagination. As an Aquarian I was fascinated by the idea of this exciting new era dawning, and wondered what the hell it had in store. Well, now we know.

In the mid sixties, at the same time a few unfortunate male actors were exposing their pale blue[1] genitals to bemused London audiences, across the Atlantic a U.S. Senate subcommittee was hearing another version of the projected Age of Aquarius. This version was to be called the Age of Leisure and its key features were forecast to be that everyone in business would soon work significantly fewer hours (maybe 20 to 25 hours a week), would work smarter (whatever that meant), and would be paid significantly more. When the Age of Aquarius dawned, what actually occurred was a massive loss of traditional jobs, a countergrowth in a whole new kind of employment, everybody

[1]It was the lighting. A very unfortunate choice of color.

working their butts off for every hour that God provides, and a handful of people getting really seriously rich. Oh, well.

What went wrong (or right, depending on your vantage point)? The rogue variable that nobody, *n-o-b-o-d-y* could predict in the sixties was the rate of growth in information technology. It blew up every assumption that seemed valid at the time and, in thirty years, changed the structure and face of business more profoundly than anything else had done in any other period in history, including the Industrial Revolution—maybe more than all of them added together.

My own thirty years in big business, all of it in white-collar supervision and management, ran parallel to this shift. Maybe 1000 years from now some archeologist will dig me up and christen me "Aquarius Man," and an anthropological study will reveal how my business life, and my approach to it, evolved over the period. I laughed louder than most at a scene in William Hurt's movie (*Love and Death on Long Island*) in which he plays a writer trying to drag himself out of a time warp of romanticism into the modern world of word processors and TV soaps. Going into a consumer electronics store, he peers intently at a row of microwave ovens and informs the assistant that, "I would like to buy one of these video recorders." There, but for the grace of God. Over the years, I worked for three major corporations, each of which had a mixed approach to technology. All of them considered it essential to be at the vanguard of production technology, but were much less sure about technology's role for management. It was often left to individual champions to lead the way in this field, but their impact was mixed, as none of those champions were in the boardroom. At the start of the 1990s if you had put a laptop on my desk, I would have thanked you and attempted to get coffee out of it. Now I use one every day, I revel in the Web, and I can produce things like: ✐ and ♣.[2]

This is not the time or the place for a history of IT developments in the Age of Aquarius, but we need to recognize the three big changes IT brought about if we are to define universal laws concerning what we have to do to win in this environment:

---

[2]I still can't find the coffee program. Is it Ctrl + F4? I can't find it in the Help software and I have been "on hold" with the IBM help desk since 1995.

The first change was the growth in technology. Whereas it may have been possible to forecast the rate of growth in data processing in the sixties, the real culture shaker has been the movement away from central processing to distributed systems and applications. In other words, while businesses still need those strange blue fridge-like things that are kept in controlled-climate offices and that have duplicate backup fridges in Seattle, the real breakthrough has taken place on your desk (or lap). This is what IBM got wrong in the eighties and Microsoft, Intel, Oracle, Compaq, Dell, and (originally) Apple got right.

It represents nothing short of an explosion of power in the hands of the individual, possibly at a remote location, to both access and analyze information. Whereas the progress in data processing decimated the white-collar clerical profession, the PC revolution all but wiped out the supervisor's job. Traditional wingspans (i.e., numbers of people reporting to a single boss) were five or six, but now frequently exceed twenty. This has had profound implications for delegation and empowerment, and the ability of individuals to realize much more of their potential and productivity—not always with the desired results, as we shall see.

The second structural change enabled the evolution of another age: Small Is Beautiful. Economies of production still make it possible for there to be giants in pharmaceuticals, weapons and aerospace, utilities and automobiles and so on, but economies of scale hardly exist in information anymore. In fact, the reverse can apply. The 1994–95 Voodoo Lounge world tour by the Rolling Stones was a complex undertaking, bigger than most businesses. It had worldwide revenues of $300 million, 250 full-time employees, 3 stage settings leapfrogging each other via 56 trucks in the U.S. (and two 747 jets and a Russian cargo plane in the rest of the world). Labor costs, travel schedules, and revenues all needed tracking, and the usual management SNAFUs occurred (fire marshals threatening to close the concert if Keith smoked on stage, which he insisted on doing). Flexibility was needed to add many extra shows. Sound familiar? A medium-complex, mid-size business? Needs a central office and an organization chart?

Policies and procedures? Naaah. Michael Cole, the Canadian concert promoter, created a glorious "virtual company" without knowing it was called that. Armed with a laptop, a portable fax, and one crate of files, he ran the whole caboodle from his tour hotel rooms.

The age of Small Is Beautiful has had dramatic effects on business. The line between home and office has blurred, even for some employees working for large corporations. Telecommuting has crept in as a habit as the majority of homes (60 to 70 percent in the U.S.) will have computers by the year 2000. The tiniest of companies (often one person) can pitch for new business looking like a major corporation, on professional-looking stationery supported by cool graphics. They can control all the lines on the operating statement and access and analyze data via a cheap modem with very little handicap compared to the big guys. These developments have had a deep impact on the traditional way we have done business. First, they have enabled, even encouraged, many corporations to outsource some of the services that used to be supplied by employees (e.g., the cafeteria, security, maintenance, computer utilities, parts of HR, and so on). Second, they have enabled thousands more women to blend professional and domestic roles in ways that couldn't have been contemplated much before 1985. A byproduct of all this is that it has become more attractive to seek a career in smaller, 3F companies (Funky, Fluid, Flexible) rather than head straight from college down the well-trodden path of an entry position with a giant.

The third change brought about by progress in IT has been the erosion of geographic (and time zone) boundaries. It is perfectly possible for one executive to run a worldwide retail operation from a U.K. base (often staying up at night to span time zones for interactive communication). Today, a feasible corporate model might include an investment base in Japan, production in South Korea, and marketing in the U.S. The impact of this has been to turn the developed Western economies, particularly in the U.K. and U.S., into service and information industry specialists. Eighty-eight percent of the

U.S. labor force is projected to be in the service sector by the year 2000, and 80 percent of U.S. management will be knowledge workers by then.

All these developments have had a mixture of "good news" and "bad news" effects. It is in banking the former and avoiding the latter that we find we need some universal laws to guide the way.

Let's start with *empowerment*, a word invented by HR because the previous words we had for it (*delegation* and *trust*) clearly weren't hip enough. The biggest gap between walk and talk in business today is in the area of empowerment. Nonetheless, the advent of distributed computing and telecommunications has allowed unprecedented levels of accountability and responsibility to be pushed down and out from the corporate nerve center, with generally positive results measured in terms of efficiency, productivity, and (to some degree) the satisfaction, fulfillment, and

**Universal Law #71**

*Good delegation is the delegated ability to succeed; bad delegation is the delegated ability to fail. They are two entirely different sciences.*

reward of those so empowered. It can go also horribly wrong, and the 1990s have provided us with a string of technically empowered rogues wreaking havoc. One of them, Nick Leeson, armed only with his PC and trading away to his heart's content in derivatives, actually brought down Baring's, one of Europe's blue chip merchant banks (which listed Queen Elizabeth among its clients[3]) from his cubicle in Singapore. The problem and the answer both lie in the fundamentals of delegation, whether it be high tech or not. Bad delegation is the delegated ability to fail; good delegation is the delegated ability to succeed. They are two *entirely different* sciences. Delegating for success chokes down on noninterference clauses, spits on machismo, and clips wings. It recognizes that success cannot be achieved on the back of a

---

[3]It's very antiroyal of me, but I find this part hilarious. I have a vision of the Queen, in the drugstore, trying to pay for her panty liners with her Baring's Visa card, and having it rejected for insufficient funds.

felony or a bluff or a heinous misjudgment. It defines appropriate audit trails and it provides relevant checks and balances. It applies game theory, minimizing the maximum damage. In short, it trusts but verifies, and the formula is different for every set of circumstances. Done correctly, it is seen by all parties as *support*, not control, but it is essential in areas where you delegate real strike power.

A second issue that has emerged during the Information Age is that of complexity. It is now well within the capabilities of an individual to make the support data and modeling for a single task so complex as to be incomprehensible to a peripheral outsider (maybe including the boss), just as it is possible for a company to create such a complex intra- and international corporate architecture that it is virtually impossible to trace legal and fiscal responsibility. In the U.K. the jury system, which originated with Henry the Second and is so treasured in our civilization, is coming under pressure because some of the (largely corporate) modern criminal trials are so complex as to be beyond the understanding of ordinary citizens pulled off the streets for jury duty. I see this complexity issue—where a bunch of information elitists put up complexity barriers to shield what they are doing—manifesting itself everywhere in business, and typified by the world of derivative investments. It is estimated that Western capitalism is now underpinned by $16 to $20 trillion (about the same value as the U.S. commercial real estate portfolio) invested in these time-machine coin tosses, many of which are so complex that it is almost impossible to value them or account for them. I see this problem mirrored in many companies, where an information complexity barrier can shield what's going on in an organizational outpost.

**Universal Law #72**

*No matter how dumb it makes you look, insist that nothing go on in your area of responsibility unless the principles are understood by you or somebody in your control tower.*

My rule is simple: I don't care how dumb it makes me look, *nothing* goes on anywhere in the business where

I have responsibility unless I or somebody in my control tower understands the principles. If you don't apply this and it goes wrong, you can look an awful lot dumber.

Another potential downside of the "fewer people, more chips and fiber optics" age is the depersonalization of business. Many businesses have eliminated telephone receptionists in favor of automated receive and direct systems, secretaries are becoming an endangered species, and it seems the only access to a human being is now via a voice mail box or E-mail address. The traditionalists are appalled. Then again, they were ticked off when the three-hour, three-martini lunch faded from the landscape along with the handshake deal, the pinstripe suit, the ability to have people thrashed when they questioned orders,[4] and the ability to keep women out of the executive suite. Poor, poor dears. Life moves on, and the good news is that these much-maligned technical developments (and I include faster, cheaper travel and facilities like teleconferencing) have made individuals more accessible than ever *if they want to be.* The answer, as always, is in the mind-set of the individual. If you want to use technology as a barrier, you can do so, just as you used to use your receptionist and secretary for the same purpose. However, if you want to be accessible you can mix technology with your physical activities in such a way that pretty much anybody on the planet can interact with you—any time, any place. *De*personalized? Business can be the most personalized it has ever been, but that relies on individuals making their mix of technology and behavior work to this end for them and their business roles.

**Universal Law #73**

*The depersonalization of business is all in the mind. All individuals in the company have the wherewithal to put together a personal mix of behavior and technology that makes them more accessible, to more people, more often than ever before. So what's stopping you?*

The naysayers aren't finished yet, though. They point out that the Information Age has made companies vulnerable to a whole new kind of crime: the ability of outsiders to steal

---

[4]Still available as a management option in Singapore and parts of New York.

**Universal Law #74**

*Your internal company information might be the nearest thing you have to precious metals in your business. Lock it up when you're not using it, and prevent unauthorized access at all times.*

data or intercept transactions, often from remote locations. Well, yes. In fact, absolutely. In just the same way, this brave new world has had to pay a lot of prices as civilization has grown, prices that include terrorism, sun-dried tomatoes, paparazzi, tofu, and country line dancing. Just as you have to do for the rest of those splinters-in-your-ass-as-you-slide-down-the-stair-rail-of-life, so you have to do with high-tech fraud: Minimize it, avoid it if you can, but recognize it exists. We are beginning to accept that assets can be intangible (well, all except the accountants) and that intellectual capital can mark up a company's stock price just as effectively as real estate, so it's not hard to take the next step. What supports intellectual capital? Information, patents, brand equity, and brains, that's what—so do your damnedest to keep them all secure, if you've got all four. With a bit of luck all companies have information; treat it as a valued resource. Remember, if it were a precious metal, you'd lock up your inventory every night. Information might just be the nearest thing to a precious metal you've got.

I've spent my time so far knocking down the moaners, but there is a concern about one aspect of the march of technology that causes me to switch sides, in fact about which I have more worries than most. Progress in this dimension of the technical revolution has been largely driven by supply-side thinking, usually by a combination of vendors and a small "center of excellence" IT team at the corporate HQ. Obviously users are consulted and involved and they are trained to take over and benefit, but development and implementation of many systems initiatives are normally handled by a central team. History is littered with the shipwrecks of systems initiatives that are launched but then fail (or at best stagnate) because of a lack of follow-through once the ribbon-cutting ceremony is over. The IT team moves on to another project, and there isn't enough expertise or demand pull to sustain the completed project. In short, three or four decades into this great age, we still have a generation of unprofessional users and a massive knowledge gap between the folks running the business and the IT Nazis.

My position on this situation is simple. If we had spent one-tenth of the money we have invested in information technology since 1965 on training our people to a level such that they could apply system solutions to daily problems and opportunities, we would be far healthier today. Supply-side IT strategies attempt to measure dumb things like "percentage of revenues spent on systems as compared to our competitors." They do not measure "average spent on IT training per potential user compared to our competitors." In my view, one is highly relevant and the other one isn't. Figure it out for yourself.

I would make training an absolute priority until a company had outspent its competitors on IT training for three years in a row. If necessary I would freeze capital spending on new generation systems until this had been achieved. Yes, I know that such training hits the income statement and doesn't sit on the balance sheet. But such a game plan would probably have the beneficial side effect of making sure a company gets the most from its current generation of systems before it pours more cash into new ones, often just because they are available. Underutilization and spare capacity in the current PC population are expensive jokes. Oh, by the

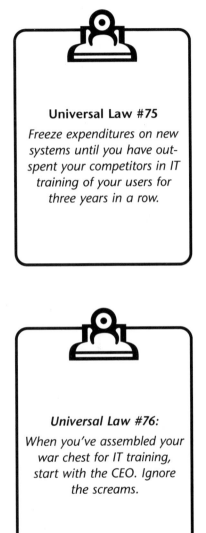

**Universal Law #75**
*Freeze expenditures on new systems until you have outspent your competitors in IT training of your users for three years in a row.*

**Universal Law #76:**
*When you've assembled your war chest for IT training, start with the CEO. Ignore the screams.*

way, a good place to start with this training (and cultural?) onslaught in many companies is with the CEO.

Now, gentle reader, we come to the intriguing subject of blame-storming. This occurs when a group of people sit down and come up with reasons why somebody (or something) else is to blame for a plan going off target, which at first glance would appear to be an embarrassing fit with their own areas of responsibility. Nothing new in this, of course; it's been going on throughout history ("I am a soldier; I was only obeying orders.") and few people could claim a completely clean record,[5] but the advent of the Information Age has elevated it to undreamed-of heights. Now we have the ability to blame-storm truly sophisticated reasons for failure. All the old standbys (cyclical distortion, inept predecessors, forces majeure, too many cutbacks, customers who just don't "get it") are capable of extensive research, and variance analysis has become a cornerstone of life in many companies. This byproduct of our brave new world is a virulent cancer and it invades the whole corporate culture if it is not stopped. Luckily, I have discovered an antidote that is very simply administered. It should apply with just as much integrity if you, yourself, are in the dock as it should if somebody else is. The rules should be chiseled in stone: For every minute you spend on the problem, spend five minutes on the proposed solution; for every minute spent on the past, spend five minutes on the future; talk about the past and problems without charts and sophisticated backup, but be as detailed as you need to be and use whatever support material you want to talk about the future and the solution. Trust me: Implement these rules and blame-storming will be history.

**Universal Law #77**

*The cure for blame-storming: Demand five minutes of talking about the solution for every one spent reviewing a problem, five on the future for every one on the past, and insist that the problem and the past are presented verbally, without sophisticated backup. Allow proposals for the future and the solution to be as detailed and well supported as necessary.*

---

[5]If year-to-year sales growth fell short for a month, my own favorite was, "Ah, yes, well, last year there were five Saturdays in the month." In one of my lesser years, if anyone had checked, the preceding year had an aggregate of seventy-two Saturdays.

If we now put some rules in place about the economics of information technology, we'll be home free. It is quite clear, as a starting point, that a great number of the massive investments in this area over the last thirty to forty years have provided astonishing returns. Both the effectiveness and efficiency of many companies have undergone unprecedented improvement. I witnessed one of the greatest with my own eyes when I was with Shell in England in the late 1960s and early 1970s. In less than a decade, virtually all retail gasoline pumps in the U.K. moved to self-service, which meant the customer had to get out of the car and go inside the shop to pay. Not only did it save labor, but the switch created a huge after-market because customers were exposed to impulse-purchase opportunities for accessories and convenience items. Today it is possible for a cash register transaction in a department store to trigger a signal in a vendor's production facility in another country, resulting in huge efficiencies in inventory control and distribution logistics.

Over this period, however, I have witnessed many investments in information technology that have not paid back, particularly when first-generation systems are replaced by a new release of hardware or software or an add-on. A myth has evolved, often perpetrated by the lethal vendor–central IT team mix, that many investments in this field bring returns that are difficult to quantify or that they trigger multiple (or complex) accountabilities and responsibilities. How do you justify the cost of a system driven by legal compliance requirements? An upgraded phone system? More relevant management information, available faster? What happens if the investment is made not to increase profit, but to slow down a decline—isn't that just as valid? The answer is quite clear today, as it should have been throughout the journey so far. The days are over when an IT rainmaker could wander about and take full ownership and responsibility on somebody else's behalf for a major system expenditure. There is no gray area, no room for compromise. Investment in information technology remains a huge opportunity for most companies and a must-do for many, but it must live and die in the same way as any other investment opportu-

nity. It does not go on the balance sheet unless there is a clearly defined projected return, with the part of the business projecting that specific return accepting ownership and accountability for its delivery. Period.

The Grateful Dead rock band is famous for a number of things, not the least of which is a guitarist who reached virtuoso standard with a finger missing.[6] Among its many other accomplishments was a song called "Trucking," which described the band's own journey together as "a long, strange trip." I can come up with no better description for the march of IT and its impact over the last thirty to forty years. It has paralleled my own tenure in business, and it has changed my approach and capability profoundly over that time. I have witnessed changes caused by IT in almost every aspect of every industry, and I am in no doubt that these developments will stand comparison with any of the great breakthroughs in history: fire, the wheel, the plow, the printing press, the steam engine, penicillin, internal combustion, the splitting of the atom, and possibly even the Wonder Bra.

The journey has confused a lot of people, and the pacing has left others uncomfortable. Many—too many—still hide their ignorance or lack of confidence behind a Luddite sneer. Luckily all of us agree about one glorious certainty in all this: When Nick Leeson (the hero who brought down Baring's Bank) scuttled from Singapore to Munich in an attempt to escape justice, he became the first fugitive in history to flee *toward* Germany.

[6]The same guy launched a best-selling range of neckties, based on the logic (I think) that he'd never worn one in his life. He then cemented his legend status by dying.

# 13

# On (Corporate) Engagements, Living Together, Marriage, and Divorce

I set out to lead a simple life. When I was two days old (I remember it clearly) I formulated my life's mission statement as follows: *Saturdays are for soccer (I'll have to watch it for a bit until I can play, then I'll play for as long as possible, then I'll watch it again), earn just more money than I will need, procreate, fifteen minutes of fame, debilitating disease, die.* Then, on the third day, I realized I wasn't going to make it until Day Four unless my mother gave me some milk, and I was introduced to life's most complicating factor—relationships.

More than fifty summers later, it is still hard to grasp the totality of how my life has been both nourished and corroded by relationships—some I've sought, some forced on me, and some pure accidents. There were those that took very little time to forge, yet lasted years. When I met my wife more than thirty years ago I knew instantly that this was the woman with whom I wished to share the rest of my bed.[1] Other personal relation-

---

[1]This line will cost me...but I can't resist it.

ships existed for almost as long a time but never entered a comfort zone. I have developed business relationships with those above, below, and alongside me. Social acquaintances have come and gone, and a limited number of lifetime friendships have evolved with the strangest bunch of people.[2] During the journey, after my wife and I merged (to use a corporate expression), we produced two new ventures (our sons) and launched them on an unsuspecting world market. On their bad days they seem to have every one of my genes in evidence; on their good days they seem to have all their mother's strengths. I guess they will carry on our brand name.

Any of this sound familiar to those of you in business? It should: Most people start businesses with a simple idea or core competency (making something or offering a service), and then realize on day three (just as I did) that relationships are going to make the whole thing complicated. This usually happens on the way back from your first visit to your bank ("Of course we'll lend you money, just as soon as you prove to us you don't need it"). As you progress on the corporate mission you find you relate to other businesses in all sorts of ways, and you develop a range of friendships, partnerships, alliances, mergers, subsidiaries, joint ventures, and strictly commercial ties. Often when you reach the corporate equivalent of fifty summers, you stop and look at it all and find that some part of the mix makes sense (and you'd like more of the same), while another part makes no sense at all. You wonder why you did what you did, and you can't remember.

GrandMet, my last company, started in business around the time I did, led by a visionary entrepreneur. Spotting the U.K. postwar real estate market opportunity, he began to build a business around marketing real estate as a core competency, starting with hotels in London (which eventually evolved into the Intercontinental group). The major U.K. brewers also held huge real estate portfolios of (linked) pubs, so it made eventual sense to acquire one of them. Okay so far? Figure this out: Over the next twenty to twenty-five years, the group acquired or

---

[2] If you put them all in one room it would appear God was having a fire sale.

allied with additional business interests in (among others): restaurants, off-track betting, packaged foods, oil, chewing tobacco, eyeglasses, and wines and spirits. It then had a kind of second marriage—to the U.S. Pillsbury and Burger King group— and proceeded to divorce its first spouse (real estate) and get rid of a few children. Internally the process was called de-cluttering, and it has been very successful. But GrandMet is still a diversified company, as are (by the *Economist*'s calculation) 80 percent of the companies listed on both the Fortune 500 and U.K. stock exchange.

Welcome to the world of corporate relationships— engagements, living together, marrying, and divorcing—and my attempt to make some sense of it.

This topic has deliberately been placed in the penultimate chapter. We are going to try to figure out a few universal laws where there just don't seem to be any, or the need for any. What works in one set of circumstances seems a recipe for failure in another, and each project seems to involve such a specific set of factors that an exercise in trying to figure out common laws seems doomed. So if I fumble the ball in this chapter, I've got one chapter left to try to recover it.

The subject is companies, or parts of companies, getting together (strategic alliances, acquisitions, joint ventures, etc.) or getting un-together (divesting, outsourcing, unbundling, etc.). One of the reasons this whole subject is confusing is that there is no single trend in evidence: There is a hell of a lot of traffic going one way (1997 had the most mergers in history) but also a hell of a lot going the other way (1998 had the most divestitures in history), all seemingly on the same highway.

Alliances of any kind in the West never seem easy, and I believe there is a background point about philosophy that we need to register before we look at examples and figure out some rules. If you get two Western executives to take a time-out from their daily grind (say at a seminar or business school) and you stand them both in a room about three feet apart, draw a line on the floor between them, and then brief them that they should each try to convince the other one to come across the line, the results are astonishing. A particular gene comes into play that causes an impasse to develop in seconds and that, if you let it play out, will find these executives entrenched for hours or even (I've heard) days, until exhaustion rules. Why? Because it is seen to be about winning and losing. Do this exercise in Japan and after a few moments one executive is likely to say, "I'll come over to your side if you'll come over to mine." Five minutes later they're back in the group, smiling. Both have won, neither has lost.[3] I don't know, but I have a feeling that if you played this game with two female executives in the West, you would get more of a Japanese-style solution.

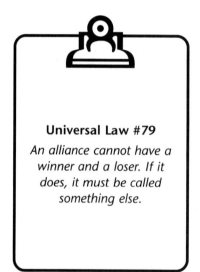

**Universal Law #79**

*An alliance cannot have a winner and a loser. If it does, it must be called something else.*

Have I personally witnessed this phenomenon? No, and it's probably a crock, but there's nothing in the introduction to this book that says I'm writing it under oath. I use that example to illustrate a point about which I *am* sure, and which I have seen evidence of a million times in U.S. and U.K. businesses—all activity is about winning and losing. I am grateful to Michael Bywater[4] for unearthing a quote from the late Myles nà Gopaleen which (although it wasn't meant to) neatly describes the role and goals of most Western capitalists: "Give a man plenty of food, beer, and the chance to score off his enemies, and you won't hear much whining out of him." That applies to most I've known and, it should be added, I've had my moments as well.

There are thousands of examples of companies coming together and coming apart. Some make sense or seem to work well, some don't. The companies involved pursue many differ-

---

[3]This is one of the reasons why everybody dislikes the Japanese. The funny thing is, they really don't know why this is, although everybody else is quite clear.

[4]From his gloriously demented book, *The Chronicles of Bargepole* (Jonathan Cape, 1992).

ent goals, which cannot all represent universal laws. But we can put a bunch of successful ventures in one pot and a bunch of missteps in another. We can then take a random handful out of each, look at them, and see if there are some universal "dos and don'ts," whatever your goals.

First one out of the good news pot: In 1998 the head of Delta Airlines must have had apoplexy when he woke up one morning to be greeted by the news of the strategic alliance between Continental Airlines and Northwest. Whatever Delta's business plan contained, it was instantly obsolete and gave God his first big laugh of that day. Here you had two players on the world airline stage, who shared only a handful of routes, seeking market synergy (Continental being strong in Europe, Northwest in Latin America and Asia). In an industry that was putting increasing pressure on costs so that companies could compete on price, it gave both parties considerable facility efficiencies through the worldwide opportunity to share airport slots. In a similar way the leaders of IBM and Hewlett-Packard, numbers one and two in the computer market, had their cornflakes ruined at about the same time by the news of Compaq's acquisition of Digital Equipment Corporation (DEC).[5] At a stroke, Compaq became a total solutions provider, adding DEC's high-end workstations and corporate servers together with its worldwide service organization and direct sales operations to the strength of its own PC base camp. Provided that Eckhard Pfeiffer, Compaq's CEO, can mask over the obvious winner or loser status of the two companies in the new entity and rekindle the motivation of DEC's shaken workforce, the map of the computer world has been irrevocably redrawn.

Eyebrows were raised when the successful Gillette Company acquired the successful Duracell Company via an exchange of stock in 1996. The sixth-leg logic—Gillette's apparent search for a sixth product group to add to razors and blades,

---

[5]Talk about a SMEF (Spontaneous Mass Existence Failure) by DEC. This would have been unthinkable a few years ago, but that's another book. Possible title? *The Decline and Fall of the Undeclineable and Infallible.* This is as far as I've gotten with this idea, and I do not expect to be killed in a rush of frenzied publishers. God, I hate Tom Clancy.

electrical appliances (Braun), toiletries and cosmetics, stationery products (Parker, Waterman pens, etc.), and toothbrushes (Oral B)—appeared stretched, but Wall Street roared its approval when Gillette sold the move as a game plan to support continued stellar growth in earnings. No dilution here, no big charges to earnings. One minute Duracell was flying solo, the next minute contributing to another load of investors, with market and distribution synergies an important but distant second. Hey, it's open and honest. Works for me.

Creating a behemoth in order to bank economies of scale (in everything from production to marketing, distribution to IT) and reduce risk in tough markets is a well-trodden path. My old Company, GrandMet, has now merged with Guinness and formed a new entity (Diageo), creating within the overall architecture a massive wines and spirits combination that is the sum of both their previous businesses in that field. One cannot help but feel wary in markets crying out for "bigger, better, fewer" worldwide brands, but when the core product (alcohol) is likely to come under more regulatory pressure, big looks kinda beautiful. Pharmaceuticals, weaponry, airlines, and telecommunications all exhibit some of the same market characteristics, and behemoths now cover the landscape in all of them.

Securing supply or distribution channels is a difficult task, but some have done it remarkably well in particular circumstances. Vertically integrating (making an alliance upstream or downstream from your own business) has also been the downfall of many. For example, many music product retailers have had great faith in their ability to be music product distributors as well, and then found out that moving trucks is a lot different from sorting shelves. There are thousands of examples when this logic has proved faulty, but some have shown it can work if the circumstances are right and the skill is there. Caterpillar's relationship with its dealer network, in which each dealer is treated as a strategic partner and not an arm's-length distribution agent, has been the key in defending its market against Japanese competition.

We used alliances to help with Burger King's urgently needed brand repositioning in the early 1990s. After developing our Kids Club, we won (a.k.a. bought) the exclusive rights (from a frankly apathetic McDonald's) for the use of the Disney name and products for our kids promotions and premium giveaways. In one stroke we legitimized our family-friendly goals. We supported this with a switch from Pepsi to Coca-Cola—the former pushing to supply us on the basis of the quality and price of its soda, the latter pushing on the basis of a total marketing and supply package (a strategic alliance in every sense). When we added these moves to all our own activities, we achieved the impossible within two years: making kids and moms comfortable in Burger King again.

Now let's switch, and reach into the "failures" pot. Ho! There are some beauties here. AT&T acquiring NCR, Kodak moving into pharmaceuticals and consumer health, and several more examples of *conglomeritis mixamatosis*. This is the disease that resulted in chewing tobacco appearing in GrandMet's portfolio—the drive to diversify by acquisition or alliance. Often the drive is fueled by a logic that identifies a weakness in the base business of a company and makes a resultant plan to offset the weakness by moving into another business about which less is known. Quite so. Japan's consumer electronics industry's entry into the Hollywood studio business is a blue-chip example of this kind of game plan in action. Although I exaggerate somewhat to make the point, the outcome is a fair representation of many others.

There are examples, however, when much stronger logic supported a corporate wedding but it still went wrong. Union Pacific's railroad merger with Southern Pacific looked like a marriage made in heaven, with $800 million worth of annual efficiencies identified as the two stood at the altar in September 1996. It is fair to say that the newlyweds got off to a rocky start, with UP's 1997 earnings down by $432 million, largely due to massive (and I mean *m-a-s-s-i-v-e*) operational problems. These in turn have had disastrous derivative effects on many businesses and utilities that rely on the combined network, and it looks like it's going to get worse before it gets better.

This is a hell of a useful example for us because pretty much all the factors that could have gone wrong did so: poor due diligence and planning (what looks obvious in principle can flounder when you get into detail); Murphy's Law (hurricanes); missteps (derailments and the odd fatal collision—hey, nobody's perfect); the government (new, more restrictive federal safety rules—spoilsports); and a glorious refusal by management to accept bad news. Pure chaos, and the unchallenged winner of my 1990s Prince Charles Bad Marriage award.

One more example out of the "bad" box gives us a different view of the ability to screw up a great idea. In 1990 executives from two of the world's great advertising agencies—Chicago's Foote, Cone and Belding and Paris' Publicis—celebrated the creation of a "broad global alliance." After a relaxing honeymoon, which seems to have lasted a whole weekend, both partners proceeded to behave in a way that competitively threatened each other and their joint venture interests. Disillusionment set in, trust was lost, and the marriage wound up in 1996 amid accusations of sustained lying and cheating. Those involved had two behavioral choices: They could either have behaved nutritively to make it work, or corrosively to make it fail. There was no middle ground. They chose the latter, and a great opportunity was lost.

What do we draw from all this? That there are six universal laws that govern getting together, that help underpin success, whatever your business goals are. I offer them in true Burger King style: If you buy five, you get the sixth free.

Now for something completely different: corporate divorces (a.k.a/ sell-offs, outsourcing, de-cluttering, unbundling, releasing stockholder value, etc.). This is what happens when you look in the mirror and don't like what you see, the way GrandMet looked at its amazingly diverse portfolio at the end of the 1980s. It took them more than five years to retrench to a position of focus and core competencies, which then enabled them to contemplate a more suitable partnership with Guinness.

How on earth do businesses get so complicated? Businesses parallel the journey we all make as individuals. Remember the simple life plan I talked about at the beginning of this chapter? It didn't happen.

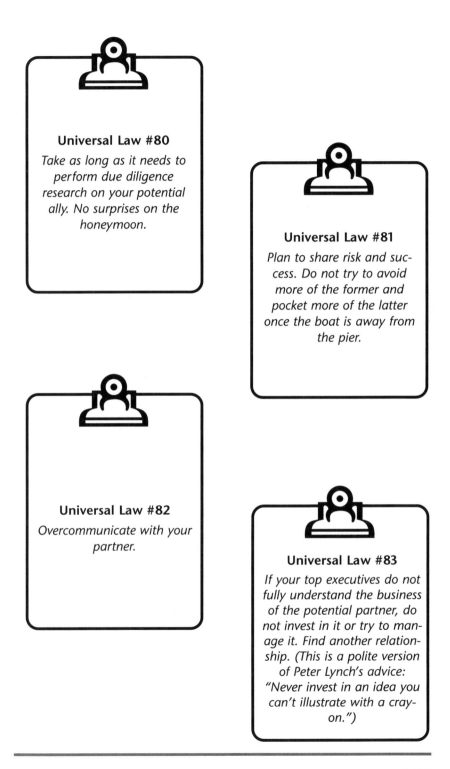

**Universal Law #80**

*Take as long as it needs to perform due diligence research on your potential ally. No surprises on the honeymoon.*

**Universal Law #81**

*Plan to share risk and success. Do not try to avoid more of the former and pocket more of the latter once the boat is away from the pier.*

**Universal Law #82**

*Overcommunicate with your partner.*

**Universal Law #83**

*If your top executives do not fully understand the business of the potential partner, do not invest in it or try to manage it. Find another relationship. (This is a polite version of Peter Lynch's advice: "Never invest in an idea you can't illustrate with a crayon.")*

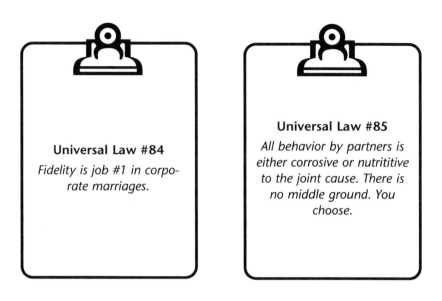

**Universal Law #84**

*Fidelity is job #1 in corporate marriages.*

**Universal Law #85**

*All behavior by partners is either corrosive or nutrititive to the joint cause. There is no middle ground. You choose.*

What did happen was that I yielded to no one in my ability to complicate my life. I set off down a simple path, with no resources, and ended up running complicated businesses in strange countries doing the weirdest things. (Selling hamburgers in Israel?)

The need to complicate things seems to invade every part of my life. I happen to like music and I like CDs. My wife and I are the only two permanent residents in our Florida home, so you'd figure that, being affluent, we might have a CD player each. You can imagine my surprise when I counted *seven* CD players in the house and cars. Seven! I have no idea how we got so many, although I attribute some of them to a theory I have about lawyers and wire coathangers: If you put two in a closet overnight, there will always be three there in the morning.

Total, over the top, unnecessary complication—and this from a guy who vowed to keep it simple. Somehow it all became unwieldy and complicated. The same thing has happened to rock stars, the language we speak, and modern business.

I grew up with rock music, and it's been fascinating to watch some of the stars who stayed the course. Almost invariably they started off simply, with a single message and a one-dimensional image. Limited by budgets and deficient concert venues in which to perform, they developed themselves through tight, live performances with one or two voices and a handful of instruments. Twenty-five years later, some of those same bands manifest themselves to their (still) adoring publics through the most complex studio recordings, supplemented by an endless parade of session musicians and singers. Videos of a single song have become big-budget, multi-image productions. Concerts are mind-blowing experiences of sound and light, often in huge stadiums that make the small, wiry, aging geyser-rockers look almost irrelevant.

Then a new need emerged—the need to get back to basics. MTV captured the concept for a generation by calling it *Unplugged* and simply doing away with all that stuff. The musicians almost seek solace in this reendorsement of their core competencies and credibility, and it usually results in strengthening their positions in the marketplace. In some cases it results in a new lease on life.

The same thing has happened with the English language. We have responded to change and development by adding new words without raking out the dead and obsolete ones. We add words like *ongoing* when we already had the perfectly adequate *continuing*. We have *empowerment* where *trust* once did the job. Somebody, who will surely rot in hell, took the concept of winning and decided to make an adjective from it, and we got *winningest*. We insist on qualifying the word *unique* (quite unique, rather unique, etc.) when it clearly can't be qualified—something either is unique or it isn't. The last sentence contained the adverb *clearly*, where it obviously wasn't needed. And as for *obviously*....

The same process has affected business, and not just through unnecessary alliances, add-ons, mergers or acquisitions. Many find ways of flying solo to the same destination. Usually rooted in a core competency and operating in a single dimension, most businesses start with a good idea executed well. Success (if it occurs) leads to growth and complication—new products, new markets, new skills, new technologies, and lots more people. Then there are government regulations and environmental and community issues to consider, and all that's *before* you decide to go for a joint venture in China.

Suddenly you find yourself trying to manage, in-house, strange competencies that aren't in your core, ranging from graphic design to office security and from travel management to feeding lots of people. Customers seem to need help buying your products, so you open a financial services business. You sensibly pursue growth by acquiring a similar business, but then find you also bought a very dissimilar business as part of the deal. But it flows cash so you decide to, well,...er, keep it. For some reason you decide to provide cars for your executives, and suddenly you're into fleet management. One of your vendors seems to be in trouble, so you acquire that business to secure supply, and suddenly you find your Monday morning management challenges—normally limited to retail-related problems—now delightfully include labor union issues from a production plant in a place you've never hear of (and probably can't even spell).

The parallels between my daft evolution, the creative explosion of rock bands, the out-of-control growth of our language, and the logical-at-the-time step curve development of many businesses are uncanny. If it walks like a duck and it quacks like a duck, it probably will taste as good as a duck if we do the same thing with it, so maybe we can steal a solution from the other theaters of this war. I am a lost cause and can offer no solution. Neither, I fear, as long as HR exists, can the language. But rock music might, and that solution is exactly what many companies are adopting to sort this mess out: *unplugging*. In reality, what is behind most reengineering, downsizing, asset sales, spin-offs, and outsourcing is the need to de-clutter and concentrate on what you do well. That's why Nike doesn't own any production facilities and why AT&T broke up into three separate businesses. It's why Lord Hanson split up his beloved conglomerate and Rand Araskog broke up ITT. In the mid 1990s General Motors, Hoecht, NTT, Novartis, Pepsico, Rhòne-Poulenc, and Westinghouse all unplugged in one way or another, and B.A.T. Industries, Philip Morris, Pearson's, and Phillips are among many others waiting in the wings. Diversity has become secondary to focus, and size has become secondary to excellence.

The four universal laws for unplugging are (he said, staring nervously at the cue card and opening the envelope):

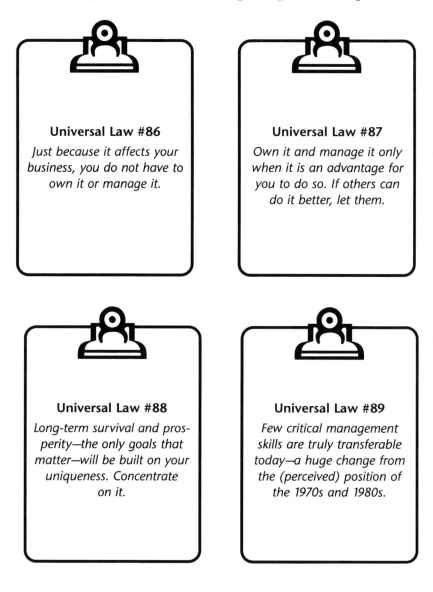

**Universal Law #86**

*Just because it affects your business, you do not have to own it or manage it.*

**Universal Law #87**

*Own it and manage it only when it is an advantage for you to do so. If others can do it better, let them.*

**Universal Law #88**

*Long-term survival and prosperity—the only goals that matter—will be built on your uniqueness. Concentrate on it.*

**Universal Law #89**

*Few critical management skills are truly transferable today—a huge change from the (perceived) position of the 1970s and 1980s.*

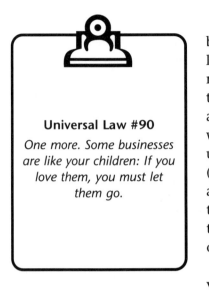

**Universal Law #90**

*One more. Some businesses are like your children: If you love them, you must let them go.*

Diversification must still exist, but not for its own sake. Size should no longer be a success criterion. Some businesses are like children: If you love them, you must let them go. Alliances and marriages will continue and many will be successful—if they follow the universal laws assembled for us (painfully) by the many who have tried and failed and (gloriously) by those who tried and triumphed. But the end of the twentieth century will mark the death of the general manager.

Tread carefully, gentle reader, as you contemplate your own company relationship strategy. The price of getting this wrong remains high, as the little ant found out when he fell in love with a female elephant. His love was not in vain and they had a glorious night of passion together, but he (the ant) woke next morning to the tragic (and large) sight of his partner lying dead. The little guy was inconsolable, not only for his lost partner but for what lay ahead for him. Through the tears he reached for his shovel, and his words still haunt us all: "I had one night of heaven, and I'll spend the rest of my life digging a grave."

# 14

# On Challenge Cultures

I'm going to start this chapter with a true story, for once. It's about a little polar bear who came home from school one day with a confused look on his face. After a while he looked up from his homework and said to his mom: "Am I *really* a polar bear?" His mother, who was busy, assured him he was and told him to get on with his study until supper was ready. Later on, when his father had got back from the office and was reading him a bedtime story, the little fellow asked if he (his dad) and his mom were also both polar bears. He was assured that was so and went to sleep. Over breakfast the next day he asked the same question about his grandparents and kept on doing so, going back a generation each time, until his dad eventually decided that enough was enough and sat him down to find out what all this was about. In a stern voice, he reaffirmed that they were all polar bears and had been throughout family history from the beginning of time. Putting on his best paternal posture, he asked his son: "Why do you keep questioning?" The little bear looked his dad in the eye and answered him straight away: "Because I am bloody freezing."

I love the little guy. He represents something I believe the business schools and the world of HR now call a "challenge culture." For once, I'm not going to get cynical about a couple of buzzwords. The reason is that the concept was actually christened by my Burger King HR lieutenant Nigel Travis (I believe after a few free champagnes on a trans-Atlantic flight), so I believe it has an honorable genesis.

The idea goes beyond new branding, which itself recognizes that virtually every employee, from chairman to janitor, can play a role in creating brand distinction. A challenge culture recognizes that all employees and stakeholders in the company can contribute to solving its problems and realizing its opportunities, but will only do so if they are motivated, capable, and comfortable in so doing. The wee polar bear felt very comfortable in challenging his parents. Something was clearly wrong in his mind; he felt he had something to say. He was obviously bright, and had worked out that he was probably a giant panda who had been mistakenly placed in the frozen Antarctic wastes, so he spoke up. He did so in the knowledge that he was not going to get taken off at the knees for challenging.

**Universal Law #91**

*A modern company needs everybody to contribute—not just to what is being done today, but to what could be done tomorrow.*

There are two (linked) concepts that must be accepted by those at the very top of the business before a company can even contemplate generating a challenge culture. First there must be a genuine acceptance that a modern company needs everybody to add value and contribute, not just to what is being done today but to what could be done tomorrow. That's tough for many senior executives to accept, because their elitist approach often precludes them from accepting that anybody else can contribute in a substantive way. After all, isn't that why they are paid the fat-cat salaries? But if that one's tough to accept, the second is even harder: For many of the issues facing the business, there is no monopoly on wisdom at the boardroom or executive committee level. In fact, in some areas, the opposite is true. In a challenge culture, a drive-through window worker in Kansas is not likely to contribute to an understanding of the problems and opportunities attending a fast food chain's contemplated joint venture in China. But for a multitude of operational issues—particularly those in the vital area of interface with the customer—the ability to contribute may well be in direct inverse proportion to the distance from the boardroom chandelier.

**Universal Law #92**

*There is no monopoly on wisdom in the boardroom. For many issues (particularly in the vital area of interface with the customer) the ability of any employee to contribute may be in direct inverse proportion to his or her distance from the boardroom chandelier.*

A challenge culture, more than anything else in business, must be led right from the top of the business. If the leader doesn't buy into these two universal laws, it's a waste of time for anybody to try doing anything about it. The challenge culture can survive in pockets here and there, and some individuals will offer glimpses of what life could be like, but unless the highest leadership works at creating a healthy climate in the corporate greenhouse, a challenge culture will not thrive.

How does a leader committed to the cause of a challenge culture go about generating it? Is it possible to institute policies, procedures, and mandates that create a culture? The answer, surprisingly, is "Yes"—but they must be accompanied by attitudes and behaviors that are nutrititive (and not corrosive) to the cause.

The first place a leader starts is with his or her own team. The science of executive recruitment has reached astonishing levels of sophistication over the past several decades, and the skills and profiles of potential candidates are analyzed in enormous detail before they are matched with a position. The process frequently includes in-depth psychological testing (of which I have never been a fan,[1] although I respect the views of many who see it as an essential element of successful recruiting). I have used a mixture of all sorts of techniques, from elongated external headhunt searches to a five-minute chat over a cup of coffee, but I have always had two tests to apply, tests I also applied to any new team members I inherited when I took over a new job. The first was that if I had any doubts, I did not make the appointment (or I removed the incumbent on an inherited team). The second was aimed at creating the genesis of a challenge culture wherever I went. Quite simply, I never hired anybody or accepted anybody in an existing team that I took over who (in my judgement) wasn't capable of hitting me. It's the antithesis of a yes-man approach, and it helps create a leadership team with a core philosophy of challenge. If you've got that, you've got a chance at developing a challenge culture. I was never actually hit during my assorted "reigns," but I have been yelled and screamed at hundreds of times. This is not a leadership approach that produces tranquility and comfort, but no other approach will get your corporate engine firing on all cylinders.

**Universal Law #93**

*Never hire anyone, or accept anyone in an existing team you inherit, who is not capable of hitting you.*

I also used my team's personal (business) objectives to reinforce a philosophy of challenge. GrandMet was a huge company that took management development very seriously, together with its attendant performance appraisals and objective setting. I often abused it, however, by sneaking in personal objec-

---

[1]This dates back to the early 1970s when I worked with Shell in the U.K. They were contemplating putting me in a sponsored master's degree program, the first time they had ever done so. As part of the process I took some psycho-tests. I'm not sure whether Shell deemed them necessary or the university, but somebody did. Part of the test was a multiple-choice paper, and one question asked if I "preferred" gardeners or cripples! I insist I am not inventing this; it is lodged in my memory, but I can't remember which box I ticked. PS: I studied for the degree at Shell's expense, passed with flying colors, and was then headhunted away. Shell dropped the program. Obviously my tests did not reveal the fact that, under my benign exterior, I was a mercenary SOB!

tives like: "You must terrify your boss at least twice a year."[2] I was making a clear point to employees: I did not see my job as constantly pushing them; sometimes it was important for me to scream in terror and pull them back from where their initiative(s) had landed them. Only then would we be getting the level of creativity, imagination, and drive we needed, but they had to know that they could go there and not die as a result. Once this was part of their approach, it permeated the business quickly.

### Universal Law #94

*All personal objectives agreed to with a boss should contain, implicitly or (preferably) explicitly, the objective of terrifying the boss at least twice a year.*

One inhibitor to the business-wide spread of a challenge culture is the existence of pockets of resistance, usually caused by some little tyrant who runs a section, unit, region, division, or whatever in line with his or her own philosophy. These people do not buy into challenge cultures, and they are powerful enough in their areas of responsibility to make sure things are run *their* way. They rule by fear, and management for them has never moved from a science of barking at subordinates to one of influencing fellow stakeholders. Admitting that somebody else—particularly somebody who is hierarchically challenged—could

### Universal Law #95

*In a healthy organization, particularly one that aspires to fostering a challenge culture, every employee should have a mentor as well as a boss.*

help the company in a way they couldn't is seen by them as a sign of weakness. It can be unpleasant working in these areas of the business, particularly if the contrast with other areas is obvi-

---

[2]I usually had a team of ten or a dozen people reporting to me, which means I should have been terrified at least twenty times a year. I usually was, but it didn't often happen via the obvious math, particularly when we had wee Gary Langstaff as our head of marketing in Burger King. He's the only guy I know who brought his approach to skiing (he used skis about half as big again as his body) to the task of brand marketing. In any one year he would terrify me enough for the whole team's aggregate. One day he will surely go to heaven, but only if St. Peter lightens up a bit.

ous. It is difficult to identify and eliminate these situations if the only line-to-management relationships that exist in these parts of the company pyramid up to the tyrant's bunker. The only real method of making sure this doesn't and can't happen is to provide an alternate route out for those trapped below decks. It's not hard to do, but it takes time and energy. The Japanese have virtually institutionalized it in their approach to management: It's known as a mentoring system.

Mentoring means that *every* person in the business has an alternate relationship with a veteran or senior figure in the company, and if it's done right both parties can benefit enormously. These relationships are not about reviewing job performance and they're not weekly relationships, but they're there if and when needed and are utilized regularly enough to perform their function. Mentoring prevents management abuse, gives the company another view of everybody, and exposes the more senior employees to another set of inputs and influences. It profoundly supports the idea and the generation of a challenge culture.

What about boring old suggestion boxes as another way of supporting a challenge culture, where anyone (remaining anonymous if they wish) can contribute their thoughts and ideas? This can facilitate rewards for the best challenges and therefore motivate people to think about new ideas in the hope they will gain personally from successful implementation. The best I can say is that I have nothing against them, provided they are handled properly. But in truth, every time I see a sign that says "Suggestion Box" I feel I'm seeing a sign that really says "Inadequate Management and Communication Processes." If they are *not* handled properly, then they move from being nutritive to being corrosive to the goal of a challenge culture. They are handled improperly when they are implemented on the back of an "It costs us nothing,

**Universal Law #96**

*Suggestion boxes cannot replace open communication and sound-sensitive management processes. If you've already got the boxes, I suggest you put plants in 'em.*

what have we got to lose" philosophy. Sure, it costs little or nothing to put a box up, but it is a bit like an employee attitude survey. Actually doing it is no big deal, but you've got to provide resources to digest and respond to the information you get in, which includes the ideas, challenges, contributions, and attitudes you get. Some of these, frankly, you'll wish you hadn't asked for. You ignore those at your peril because a lot of eyes will be watching. Suggestion boxes cannot replace open communication and sound-sensitive management processes.

So there are some mechanisms that can help institutionalize a challenge culture, but they run a poor second to the impact that can be made by behavioral leadership of the right kind. For the hierarchically challenged to feel as comfortable as our little polar bear did in standing up and making a point, they need to feel peer-group comfort with their leaders. For a leader to be able to create that comfort level, maybe down through four or five levels of the organization, takes a particular talent (yes, t-a-l-e-n-t) and style. Even if that atmosphere is created, the challengers need access and opportunity to challenge.

The equality thing is a hot button in business, so some top-level executives now insist on working out of a cubicle while others hang onto the high-life trappings of power. But the debate for the purposes of generating a challenge culture is more subtle than that. It is not about the creation of a phony equality. It *is* about the avoidance of a corrosive "us and them" atmosphere.

It was pretty easy to figure out the rules for equality in business when I first started out in big-company life, a sensitive, pale underachiever with no credit rating. We followed the universal rule as defined by George Orwell in his biting but pedestrian satire, *Animal Farm*: that all men are created equal, but some are more equal than others. The more equal got more windows in their offices.

It was easy. We all knew how it worked and frankly, it wasn't difficult to live with. Studs Terkel rationalized it nicely for us: "We have accepted—always—that the man behind the mahogany desk is better than we are."

Then the lines began to blur. Women's impact on business increased dramatically, so the law became: All persons are created equal, but some etc., etc. Equality became sexually diverse and we were all the better for it. Then it began to get really confusing. A new band of business leaders appeared on the radar screen and began acting really weird: Instead of big offices and expensive furniture, they chose to have the same facilities as everybody else. They dressed in the same way and shared the same cafeteria. They flew coach class instead of having corporate jets at their disposal and they didn't take a stretch limo to the bathroom. Wow.

What the hell was all this about? Was a real trend identifying itself? Was it of substance, or just tokenism? More important, was business going to be better off because of it?

A classic example of some being "more equal than others" is usually found in a company's air travel policy, and it's worth looking at a couple of Big Cheese examples to see what we can learn. Let's start with Sam Walton, who built Wal-Mart from scratch and overtook Sears within his working lifetime. Here's a guy who had a corporate jet at his personal beck and call—by any calculation, an extreme extravagance, costing millions of dollars that could have dropped to the bottom line.

Now let's put a more modernist leader under the microscope—Hatin Tyabji, CEO of the Verifone company, which has posted twelvefold growth within the last decade and now employs more than 2500 people. No corporate jet for this fella, yet he flies over 400,000 miles a year. He flies coach class unless he uses his frequent flyer miles for an upgrade—the same policy that applies to everyone in the company.

Okay, two very different approaches. Which is better for modern business? Is one more relevant for a challenge culture? The answer is complicated, and you may want to start taking notes here, because *both* of them are wonderful examples of what's needed. Beneath the seemingly enormous philosophical differences, these two guys have one fundamental in common: They are not interested in the trappings of power as ends in themselves, they are interested in them only as means to an end. The end is doing their jobs to the best of their ability, inspiring their people, and providing sound-sensitive management processes.

What I didn't tell you about Sam was that his office was austerity defined and he drove a pickup truck. But he saw his role, at a time in life when most folks have retired, as an endless and exhausting personal presence in his stores all over America—listening to, challenging, shouting at, smiling at, pushing and pulling his people to beat Sears' people, but above all listening and digesting challenges.

Now ask Tyabji why he doesn't have a corporate jet and the response hits you right between the eyes: "I'm not interested in making life simple. I'm interested in being a leader. You can't have emotion if you behave differently from your people."

Two very different styles but a common, admirable goal. It's when that goal becomes a mix of ego, self-aggrandizement, and status worship that the problems start: when the style factors take over from the substance, when the greed for life's luxuries, paid for by somebody else, takes over from the need to do the best possible job for the company's stakeholders. Hey, CEOs are already (and let's assume quite rightly) being paid up the wazoo in recognition of their responsibilities. If they want the sweet life, they should pay for it.

My epiphany came during a recent lunch I had with my old jamming pal TAFKAP (The Artist Formerly Known As Prince, although known to me as Squiggle after his new signature). We got close when I was a session dancer on the video for *Purple Rain,*[3] and the little guy pops round to see me quite often. We were splitting a Whopper recently and I asked him about his name change. His answer was along the lines that he felt he was "more equal" than other musicians. He was of a higher class and of a different caliber, and felt this ought to be recognized. At this juncture, I realized with blinding clarity that this kind of action, so prevalent in business as people respond to the potential privilege that can come with elevation and leadership, simply makes you look like an industrial-strength bonehead.

---

[3]I was the one who looked like a cross between Michael Jordan and Grace Jones. Each day I was approximately fifteen hours in makeup.

So, what's the rule here? Well, it's the water barrel rule, because what we're talking about are discretionary costs for a company. Costs such as rent, interest, and salaries (to a degree) are not discretionary; they are fixed in the short term. Most of the costs associated with the trappings of office are discretionary. In this tough, competitive world of low organic growth, discretionary costs are like the water barrel on a Spanish galleon making an Atlantic crossing in the fifteenth century—*precious*. If you fill a cup and drink it, that water is gone—it is not available for anyone else. So every cup has to be treasured, because the journey is long and uncertain and supplies are limited and finite. Everybody watches, and they know what's going on.

**Universal Law #97**

*Do not spend more on the lifestyle and trappings of your job than you need to do it effectively and efficiently. Spend more, and you'll create an "us and them" culture.*

So the rule[4] is: Don't take more than you need for your job, and don't take more than your share. The rule applies to everybody, from the powder monkey to the captain. It's an excellent code by which to judge your own office overhead and corporate lifestyle.

Establishing that the attitude and behavior of those at the very top of the business is essential in the creation of a challenge culture is all very well, but unless they can make themselves practically accessible to the company's stakeholders, the whole idea risks being stillborn. Providing that access is hard to do, even with the best will in the world, because the pressures of modern leadership can cheerfully eat up twenty-five hours of every day and leave little room for unstructured calendar time to meet, talk with, listen to, and respond to a bunch of folks who just might have a good idea but are far more likely to challenge you with stuff you'd really rather not hear. It's even tougher if you run a production plant

[4]To think, this wisdom was inspired by TAFKAP. Just imagine what I will come up with when I review my relationship with TAFKADK (The Alien Formerly Known As Don King).

with a few thousand hourly unionized workers or a business that's spread over fifty countries and twenty-four time zones.

There is no single technique or practice that can handle the whole job for everybody, but it's pleasing to note that technology, used wisely, has made the most difficult of these circumstances a sight more easy. Whatever the mix of techniques you use, however, the oft-documented MBWA (Management by Wandering Around) has to play a part—as big a part as you can allow it to. Sam Walton had this fixed at about 90 percent of his management mix (a style that necessitates strong lieutenants back at the home office). On the other hand, I've worked directly with a boss who had to be dragged screaming into any situation that smelled of unstructured exposure or access. Those two represent polar ends of the spectrum in my experience and as I remember it, Sam was extraordinarily successful while the other guy is now in the corporate equivalent of a pauper's grave. A note of warning, though: The purpose of all these techniques of accessibility is not to enjoy yourself or to appear cool; the purpose is to create a sound-sensitive management process (SSMP), with the overall goal of establishing a challenge culture.

In my own wanderings about, I followed two rules: First, if I knew there was a pocket of discontent, I made straight for it. I couldn't always solve it (some were frankly insoluble), but by investing my time in the discomfort zone I signaled that at least I understood the issue as defined by those who were doing the challenging, and that at best I took some ownership of the challenge

**Universal Law #98**

*Making yourself accessible as a leader is not about enjoying yourself or appearing cool. It is about creating a sound-sensitive management process.*

**Universal Law #99**

*A good rule for wandering about: If you are aware of a pocket of discontent, head straight for it.*

and there was a line of interest and communication open to me. My second rule was to start wandering at the farthest point from the boardroom chandelier and then work back. If I was visiting a franchisee in a distant region, I would start by visiting restaurants. When I started at a restaurant, I started with the lowest paid part-timer. The business sure looks different from that vantage point.

The good news today is that the wandering manager can for once be strongly supported by new technology in his or her quest to support a challenge culture. E-mail and voice mail are still pilloried by leadership Luddites as "impersonal" and "not the done thing" for captains of industry. What a crock. I agree that they are abused in business life (particularly voice mail, which now has a normal role as a hugely expensive answerphone system), but they can provide an enormously effective open communication channel to a leader who is committed to a sound-sensitive management process. This technology is not instead of, it is as well as wandering about. Bill Gates spends time every day personally answering his E-mail—at the same time giving off a magnificent signal about his openness and accessibility (and with it the culture of Microsoft).

At Burger King I used voice mail to great effect, and fell on the idea almost by accident. Our headquarters was hit by Hurricane Andrew in 1992, and for a traumatic period we lost our offices (as well as many employees losing their homes). We also lost all that good stuff we identify with normal daily business life, including our phone system. We published two phone numbers to all our employees who could be reached by cellular phones, one for them to call in with any information they felt would be relevant and helpful, and one to hear a (nightly) recorded message from me telling folks what was going on and giving status reports. It took about two minutes for somebody to christen this "BK Radio." When the world returned to normal (voice mail was back), I kept BK Radio alive, switching to a 5-minute recorded voice mail message to all corporate employees once a week. I avoided nothing and told 'em good news and bad. I lightened parts of it, poking fun at myself and others on my executive team. But the most important aspect wasn't the message going out; the most important part was that everybody who received it had the (voice mail) facility to punch a number and *reply*. I listened to every reply (150 from one broadcast), and it was gold dust for me—I learned more about what our people really thought, what concerned them, and what they wanted to challenge than I could have with a solid month's wandering about. The universal rule that applies here is that we were born with two eyes, two ears, and one mouth. That's four organs to receive information and one to give it out. That's a pretty good ratio to work with for a sound-sensitive management process, and (roughly) the opposite of what most executives feel is an effective communication mix.

> **Universal Law #101**
> *Your god gave you two eyes, two ears, and one mouth. That's four organs to receive information and one to give it out. That's a good ratio for a challenge culture.*

This hasn't been an easy chapter for me to write, because I am acutely aware of my reputation as one of the great postindustrialist populist executives of all time. This was particularly true of my relationship with the U.S. Burger King franchisees, whose open affection for me knew no bounds. Frequently when I would visit them in their regions, they would organize a local daily holiday and close the schools, garland the streets with flowers, and often sacrifice a goat or two (occasionally perhaps even a maiden). It was always difficult to hear myself over the continuous cheering, and I damaged many suits of clothes by being carried shoulder high to a banquet in my honor. Also, they never failed to introduce me to their mascot: a small, puzzled-looking, young polar bear.

# Epilogue: January 13, 2015

What happened to some of the personalities in this book?

*Steve Jobs* left Apple eleven years after starting the search for his successor and opened a fashion house in Milan. *Anita Roddick* closed the last Body Shop and started a women's professional baseball league in England. *Albert Dunlap* saw the face of Christ in his breakfast cereal one morning and gave away all his wealth to run a small abbey in Andalucia. *Van Morrison* quit singing and turned to writing, surprising the world with *Beyond Prozac*, the first blockbuster novel of the new millennium.

*Tom Peters* joined the last vestiges of Crosby, Stills, Nash, and Young for a rousing series of corporate conferences. Scarred by the bankruptcy of AutoNation, *H. Wayne Huizenga* acquired a small island (New Zealand) and retired on it. *Michael Eisner* failed in his bid for the U.S. presidency in 2008 and opened a chain of lap-dancing clubs in Argentina. Nike signed a ten-year sponsorship deal with NASA, and *Phil Knight* personally led the first interplanetary marketing drive (sneaker production was farmed out to the low-cost planet, Jordan).

*Margaret Thatcher* completed the third volume of her autobiography (*The Mad Cow Years*) and accepted an offer to become queen of the Western Province in southern Africa. *Richard Branson* collaborated with *Andrew Lloyd Webber* and launched a new Broadway musical, *Hot Air*. It closed after a week.

*The author* celebrated a string of successful business books, including *Yearnings for Earnings, Can We Do That?, In Search of Mediocrity,* and *Is That a Microchip or Are You Just Pleased to See Me?* He retired from public life after selling the movie rights to his life story (tentatively entitled *A Boomer's Tale*). At press time, *Brad Pitt* had agreed to star.

# INDEX